Good Housekeeping

400
CALORIE
VEGETARIAN

Good Housekeeping

400 CALORIE

VEGETARIAN

Easy Mix-and-Match Recipes for a Skinnier You!

HEARST BOOKS
New York

ALL RECIPES
· GOOD ·
HOUSEKEEPING
Since ★ 1909
COOKBOOKS
Triple TESTED

HEARST BOOKS
New York

An Imprint of Sterling Publishing
387 Park Avenue South
New York, NY 10016

GOOD HOUSEKEEPING
Rosemary Ellis
EDITOR IN CHIEF

Courtney Murphy
CREATIVE DIRECTOR

Susan Westmoreland
FOOD DIRECTOR

Samantha B. Cassetty, MS, RD
NUTRITION DIRECTOR

Sharon Franke
KITCHEN APPLIANCES &
FOOD TECHNOLOGY DIRECTOR

Book design: Memo Productions
Cover design: Jon Chaiet
Project editor: Sarah Scheffel
Photography credits on page 158

The Good Housekeeping Cookbook Seal guar-
antees that the recipes in this cookbook meet
the strict standards of the Good Housekeeping
Research Institute. The Institute has been a source
of reliable information and a consumer advocate
since 1900, and established its seal of approval in
1909. Every recipe has been triple-tested for ease,
reliability, and great taste.

www.goodhousekeeping.com

For information about custom editions, special
sales, and premium and corporate purchases,
please contact Sterling Special Sales at 800-805-
5489 or specialsales@sterlingpublishing.com.

Distributed in Canada by
Sterling Publishing
c/o Canadian Manda Group, 165 Dufferin Street
Toronto, Ontario, Canada M6K 3H6

Distributed in Australia by
Capricorn Link
(Australia) Pty. Ltd.
P.O. Box 704, Windsor, NSW 2756, Australia

Manufactured in China

2 4 6 8 10 9 7 5 3 1

Sterling ISBN: 978-1-61837-058-7

CONTENTS

290
CALORIES
Tomato Tarte Tatin
(page 95)

FOREWORD

At *Good Housekeeping*, we include simple and delicious vegetarian options in every issue. In *400 Calorie Vegetarian*, we've gathered our most popular meatless mains and sides, along with tips on how to stay slim the healthy vegetarian way. Each recipe is 400 calories or less and includes complete nutritional information. Icons indicate vegan, heart-healthy, and high-fiber recipes, as well as thirty minute or less and make-ahead dishes. Whether you're a vegetarian or just want to eat more wholesome meatless meals, this book is for you!

We open with recipes for delicious veggie burgers, burritos, pizza, and other fare you can eat without a fork. Then it's on to comforting soups and stews, from Gazpacho with Cilantro Cream to Red Chili with Fire-Roasted Tomatoes. Our stuffed, stacked, and stir-fried dishes lend a sense of play to mealtimes: Choose from Green Tomato Stacks, Stuffed Portobellos, Fast Fried Rice, and then some. We've also included fresh takes on pasta and grain dishes to keep things interesting: Try our Spaghetti with Beets and Greens and Summer Tomato Risotto, which is made with ease in the microwave. And why not enjoy vegetarian breakfast specialties around the clock? Our Crustless Tomato-Ricotta Pie and California Breakfast Wrap would be equally good morning, noon, or night.

To make meal planning easy, the second half of the book includes recipes for salads and sides that are brimming with vegetables and grains, plus a chapter that celebrates fruity desserts. Add-ons like Kale Chips, Crunchy Peanut Broccoli, and Double Cornbread are perfect for rounding out your meals, while treats like our Watermelon Slushies and Apple-Oat Crisp ensure a sweet and fruit-filled finale. See "Healthy Vegetarian Meal Planning" on page 9 for tips on how to create satisfying low-cal vegetarian menus—breakfast, lunch, and dinner. For advice on key ingredients, including nondairy substitutes for those who use them, see "The Vegetarian Pantry" on pages 12 to 15.

SUSAN WESTMORELAND
Food Director, *Good Housekeeping*

INTRODUCTION

Whether you're already following a vegetarian diet or are just beginning to explore what it means to eliminate meat from your meals, the health benefits are compelling. In study after study, it's been shown that a vegetarian diet rich in fruits, vegetables, whole grains, and legumes and low in fat results in numerous health benefits: It can reduce the risk of some cancers, lower the incidence of diabetes, decrease the possibility of stoke and heart disease, and have a positive effect on the health of those who already have heart disease. Furthermore, a balanced low-calorie vegetarian diet can help you lose weight or maintain a healthy weight: Enter *Good Housekeeping 400 Calorie Vegetarian*.

A good vegetarian diet is filled with fresh vegetables and fruits and nutrient-rich, fiber-packed whole grains and beans, which makes it a natural subject for our 400 calories (or less!) series. In this volume, we share more than 50 recipes for delicious meat-free mains, from yummy sandwiches to hearty soups and stews, playful stuffed, stacked, and stir-fried vegetable entrées and satisfying pastas, casseroles, and grain dishes, plus a chapter that invites you to enjoy breakfast favorites any time of day. You'll find low-cal, vegetarian takes on familiar dishes like burgers, pizza, burritos, and lasagna, plus tasty recipes that feature veggies, grains, and tofu in new ways.

As the title of the book promises, every main dish is 400 calories or less, and as a bonus, we've included chapters on vegetable and grain side dishes plus fruity desserts that will help you round out your meals in healthy vegetarian style. The 40 add-on recipes are organized by calorie count—from lowest to highest. Simply choose your entrée, then use your surplus calories to select an add-on (or two) that will make it a meal.

If you're watching your weight and limiting dinners to around 500 calories total, you could begin with Artichokes with Creamy Lemon Sauce for dipping (145 calories), enjoy our Stuffed Portobellos (290 calories, pictured opposite) as your main dish and finish with an orange: 145 + 290 + 60 = a 495-calorie meal. With *Good Housekeeping 400 Calorie Vegetarian*, it's easy to build meat-free meals that are both satisfying *and* low calorie. See "Healthy Vegetarian Meal Planning," opposite, for examples.

HEALTHY VEGETARIAN MEAL PLANNING

Planning healthy, low-calorie vegetarian brunches, lunches, and dinners is a breeze with *400 Calorie Vegetarian*. Prepare the add-ons we've suggested under "Make It a Meal" with each main-dish recipe to make 500-calorie dinners, 400-calorie lunches, or 300-calorie breakfasts. Or get creative and choose from the veggie, grain, and dessert recipe lists on pages 107, 123, and 137 to make your own satisfying meal combos. Here are some tasty examples to get you started.

SAMPLE BRUNCH MENU

MAIN: Crustless Tomato-Ricotta Pie	190 calories
ADD-ON 1: Mesclun with Pears and Pumpkin Seeds	100 calories
ADD-ON 2: One cup coffee with 1½ tablespoons skim milk	10 calories
Total calories per meal	**300 calories**

SAMPLE LUNCH MENU

MAIN: Vegetarian Souvlaki	390 calories
ADD-ON: Kale Chips	15 calories
Total calories per meal	**405 calories**

SAMPLE DINNER MENU

MAIN: Stuffed Acorn Squash	250 calories
ADD-ON 1: Green Beans with Mixed Mushrooms	80 calories
ADD-ON 2: Stuffed Fresh Figs	170 calories
Total calories per meal	**500 calories**

STAYING SLIM THE VEGETARIAN WAY

You might think that a vegetarian diet is guaranteed to keep you skinny. But consider this: most French fries, cookies, and a lot of greasy takeout foods are vegetarian. To cultivate a low-calorie vegetarian diet that's wholesome, too, follow these guidelines.

• **Think seasonal.** When vegetables and fruits are in season, they're also at their most flavorful, abundant, and affordable—thus easy to transform into mouthwatering meals.

• **Bulk up.** Switching to a high-fiber diet can be a bit like taking a magic weight-loss pill: Fiber swells a little in your stomach, which quells hunger. Fiber is also low cal: Your body can't break it down, so it runs right through your system, providing only bulk. That's several good reasons to add fiber-rich, fill-you-up whole grains and legumes to your diet. Try some options that may be new to you like bulgur, wheat berries, or millet. Recipes containing all three—and many other wholesome whole grains—are sprinkled throughout this book.

• **Explore meat alternatives.** In addition to legumes, you can add protein to a vegetarian diet with tofu, tempeh, and textured vegetable protein (TVP). Our Fast Fried Rice (page 64) is an example of an easy way to use tofu. See pages 13–15 for information about meat alternatives made from soybeans.

• **Get technique-savvy:** Use high heat to alter a veggie's flavor. Grilling, roasting, and baking can take out the bite or boost the sweetness of vegetables. Our grilled Portobello Pesto Burger (page 32) and baked Vegetable Cobbler (page 82) are two flavorful examples.

• **Go for bold.** Tweak the taste of your dishes with zingy flavor boosters like chile peppers, mustard, or olives. It pays to get to know your spice cabinet and condiment options. Sweet-and-Sour Unstuffed Cabbage (page 65) is seasoned with fresh ginger, garlic, rice vinegar, and soy sauce, while Red Chili with Fire-Roasted Tomatoes (page 46) gets its zip from chipotle chiles, cumin, and oregano.

• **Eat fruit for dessert.** Berries, bananas, peaches, and citrus are naturally sweet and filled with vitamins and antioxidants. Instead of making chocolate cake a habit, sample the luscious fruit-based desserts in our Sweet & Fruity Treats chapter (page 137).

THE VEGETARIAN PANTRY

The following foods are essential to great vegetarian cooking. Get familiar with these nutritious ingredients, and you'll be well on your way to creating delicious, satisfying, low-calorie vegetarian meals.

Beans and other legumes: Whether you choose black beans, garbanzos, pintos, cannellini, lentils, or split peas, they are packed with protein and insoluble and soluble fiber. Insoluble fiber helps promote regularity and may stave off such digestive disorders as diverticulosis. Soluble fiber can reduce LDL cholesterol levels and help control blood-sugar levels in people with diabetes. Beans are also high in saponin, a cancer-fighting plant compound. We incorporate a wide variety of beans and legumes in recipes throughout this book, so you can easily get your daily dose of this energy-giving protein.

Barley: Barley is the oldest grain in cultivation. The fiber in barley is especially healthy; studies indicate it may be even more effective than oat fiber in lowering cholesterol. Our Peach, Cucumber, and Barley Salad (page 128) is a delicious way to get to know this grain.

Cornmeal: This is ground hulled yellow or white corn; the fine-grind type is used for cornbread, while medium-grind is used in polentas, like our easy Polenta Lasagna (page 77). Choose a water- or stone-ground cornmeal; both processes leave more of the bran and germ intact.

Couscous: Originally from North Africa, this grainlike pasta is made from semolina wheat flour. The packaged, precooked version is ready to eat in just five minutes and is widely available in supermarkets. Look for whole-wheat couscous, which is similar in taste and texture to regular couscous, but packs a whopping 8 grams of fiber per serving. And see Couscous Four Ways (page 133) for delicious ideas on how flavor it.

Millet: Although we typically cultivate this cereal grass for birdseed and fodder, it is a staple in Asia and Africa. It's best toasted, then prepared like rice to make seasoned pilafs, like our Southwestern-flavored Millet with Corn and Green Chiles (page 129) or hot cereal.

Quinoa: This is another grain that, botanically speaking, isn't a grain; rather, quinoa (pronounced KEEN-wah) is a relative of Swiss chard and beets. High in B vitamins, it is also a complete protein, containing all of the essential amino acids the body can't produce itself. Shaped a lot like a sesame seed, quinoa has a crunchy-melting quality. To remove any traces of bitterness, rub quinoa under cold running water, then rinse until the water is clear before cooking it.

Oats: Oats contain a type of fiber, beta-glucan, that studies have shown to help reduce cholesterol levels. Steel-cut oats are the whole oat kernels with only the inedible outer chaff removed, cut into pieces. They are chewy but have a wonderful nutty-sweet flavor. Rolled oats, or old-fashioned oats, are whole oats that have been rolled into flat flakes then steamed and lightly toasted.

Rice: Whenever possible, choose brown rice; it's processed to remove only its inedible outer husk, leaving its nutritive powers intact. It is rich in fiber, an excellent source of manganese (a mineral that helps produce energy from protein and carbohydrates), and a good source of magnesium (helps build bones) and selenium (key to a healthy immune system). Brown rice can be long-, medium-, or short-grain.

Wheat: Wheat is a nutritional powerhouse, containing thirteen B vitamins, vitamin E, protein, and essential fatty acids. Wheat berries, the unmilled kernels of wheat, are nutty tasting and very chewy. If you've never cooked them before, sample our Wheat-Berry Salad with Dried Cherries (page 126). Bulgur is quick-cooking cracked wheat that has been parboiled and dried. You can also enjoy the whole-grain goodness of wheat in the form of whole-wheat flour, which is made from whole hard wheat berries.

Tofu: Soybean curd that is drained and pressed in a process similar to cheese-making. The creamiest tofu (with the least liquid pressed out) is called soft or silken. Use it in shakes, dressings, and dips. Extracting still more liquid produces regular tofu, then firm, and finally extra-firm tofu, which are all excellent grilled or in stir-fries. Avoid bulk tofu, unpackaged blocks sold in water; it can be contaminated with bacteria. Sealed water-packed tofu and the aseptically packaged kind (unrefrigerated) are safer. To store tofu after opening the package, cover it with cool water and refrigerate it for up to 1 week, changing the water daily.

VEGAN DAIRY AND EGG SUBSTITUTES

If you've decided to follow a vegan diet (eliminating all animal foods from your diet) or just want to eat less dairy, here's a list of some of the dairy- and egg-alternative products available today. Once only sold at health-food stores and online, today you can find many of these items in large supermarkets. Take a look in your local grocery store—you may be surprised to see the vegan products they stock.

• Nondairy margarine, including soy margarine (try Earth Balance brand)

• Soy milk, rice milk, and nut milks (including almond and cashew milk)

• Nondairy soy sour cream and cream cheese

• Nondairy yogurts made with rice, soy, almond, or coconut milk

• Nondairy soy- or coconut-milk creamers

• Nondairy soy frozen yogurt

• Nondairy ice creams made with soy or coconut milk

• Nondairy chocolate (with the exception of unsweetened cocoa powder, chocolate usually contains milk solids)

• Egg-free soy mayonnaise (try Vegenaise brand)

• Egg replacements (check vegan and vegetarian websites for recommended substitutions)

To make it easy for vegans to cook from *400 Calorie Vegetarian*, we've included a vegan icon Ⓥ in the nutritional information for all recipes that do not contain any animal products. In addition, with a little practice, you can adapt many of the other recipes in this book by swapping in the dairy and egg substitutes listed above. Experiment until you find the nondairy products you like best. Flavors and textures vary from brand to brand and also depend on what ingredient is used as the base. You may discover that you don't care much for soy-based products but adore anything made with nut or coconut milk. Or find that you love one type of nondairy yogurt for baking, while another is just the thing for a snack.

To prepare tofu for cooking, drain it and wrap it in a clean dish towel. Place the wrapped tofu on a pie plate, top it with a dinner plate, and weight it down to extract excess water. (One or two heavy cans make good weights for this purpose.) Let the tofu sit under weight for about 15 minutes.

Tempeh: A dense, chewy cake made from cooked, fermented soybeans. Like other soy products, tempeh absorbs the flavor of the ingredients it's cooked with, even though it has a smoky flavor of its own. Tempeh is sold refrigerated or frozen; try it in soups or stir-fries. Once only available in health-food stores, today you can find it in most supermarkets.

Textured vegetable protein (TVP): Also known as textured soy protein, these dried granules made from defatted soy flakes have to be rehydrated before cooking. Commercially, TVP is used to make soy veggie burgers, sausages, and hot dogs. You can find it in health-food stores and some supermarkets.

Vegetables and fruits: Eating a variety of fresh vegetables and fruits is an important part of any healthy vegetarian diet (and a good way to keep your meals skinny, too). A colorful diet filled with reds, yellows, oranges, and greens helps ensure that you get the widest range of vitamins and phytochemicals, the natural pigments in produce that help keep your body healthy. The recipes in this book offer dozens of fresh new ways to prepare veggies; see the Stuffed, Stacked, and Stir-Fried chapter (page 53) for some particularly creative takes.

MEATLESS MAINS

To make skinny vegetarian meal planning a cinch, each main dish is paired with suggestions for add-on recipes that will make it a meal. Or to choose your own add-ons, see the complete recipe lists in the second half of the book, conveniently organized by calorie count, from lowest to highest: Snacks, Sides & Salads, page 107; Get Your Grains, page 123; and Sweet and Fruity Treats, page 137.

345
CALORIES

Portobello Pesto
Burgers
(page 32)

PIZZAS, BURGERS & SANDWICHES

If you're still new to a vegetarian diet, you may be wondering: What's pizza without pepperoni? Can my family give up burgers? The yummy, low-calorie recipes that follow are your answer. We offer three irresist-ible meat-free pizzas prepared on the grill for extra flavor. And our black bean and portobello burgers are so satisfying, no one will miss the meat. If you're hankering for Mexican, try our Vegetarian Tacos or Grilled Vegetable Burritos. For lovers of pulled chicken or pork sand-wiches, we offer barbecued tofu sandwiches—so easy and delicious.

KEY TO ICONS

◔ 30 minutes or less   Ⓥ Vegan   ♥ Heart healthy   ❀ High fiber   ▤ Make ahead

GREEK SALAD PITAS

Making hummus—the Middle Eastern spread made with mashed garbanzo beans—is fast work when you use a food processor or blender.

TOTAL TIME: 20 MINUTES

MAKES: 4 SANDWICHES

1   CAN (15 TO 19 OUNCES) GARBANZO BEANS (CHICKPEAS), RINSED AND DRAINED

¼   CUP PLAIN NONFAT YOGURT

1   TABLESPOON OLIVE OIL

2   TABLESPOONS FRESH LEMON JUICE

½   TEASPOON SALT

¼   TEASPOON COARSELY GROUND BLACK PEPPER

¼   TEASPOON GROUND CUMIN

1   GARLIC CLOVE, PEELED

4   (6- TO 7-INCH) WHOLE-WHEAT PITAS

3   CUPS SLICED ROMAINE LETTUCE

2   MEDIUM TOMATOES (6 TO 8 OUNCES EACH), CUT INTO ¼-INCH PIECES

1   MEDIUM CUCUMBER, PEELED AND THINLY SLICED

1½   OUNCES FETA CHEESE, CRUMBLED (⅓ CUP)

2   TABLESPOONS CHOPPED FRESH MINT LEAVES, PLUS ADDITIONAL MINT LEAVES FOR GARNISH

1   In food processor with knife blade attached, or in blender, combine beans, yogurt, oil, lemon juice, salt, pepper, cumin, and garlic; puree until bean mixture is smooth.

2   Cut off top third of each pita to form a pocket and reserve tops for another use. Use half of bean mixture to spread inside pockets.

3   Combine lettuce, tomatoes, cucumber, feta, and chopped mint; fill pockets with mixture. Top with remaining bean mixture and garnish with mint leaves.

335 CALORIES   **PER SERVING.** 15G PROTEIN | 52G CARBOHYDRATE | 9G TOTAL FAT (2G SATURATED) 11G FIBER | 10MG CHOLESTEROL | 910MG SODIUM

MAKE IT A MEAL: Serve this sandwich with Spring Pea Dip with Veggies (page 109; 50 calories) for a fresh and healthy 385-calorie lunch.

VEGETARIAN SOUVLAKI

This vegetarian take on a traditionally meat-centered sandwich is just as satisfying as the original. Make the filling by cutting up your favorite veggie burgers. Swap in whole-wheat pitas for even more fiber.

ACTIVE TIME: 20 MINUTES · **TOTAL TIME:** 25 MINUTES
MAKES: 4 SANDWICHES

1 TABLESPOON OLIVE OIL

1 LARGE ONION (12 OUNCES), CUT IN HALF AND THINLY SLICED

4 FROZEN VEGETARIAN SOY BURGERS (10- TO 12-OUNCE PACKAGE), CUT INTO 1-INCH PIECES

¼ TEASPOON GROUND BLACK PEPPER

½ TEASPOON SALT

1 CONTAINER (8 OUNCES) PLAIN NONFAT YOGURT

1 SMALL ENGLISH (SEEDLESS) CUCUMBER (8 OUNCES), CUT INTO ¼-INCH DICE

1 TEASPOON DRIED MINT

1 SMALL GARLIC CLOVE, CRUSHED WITH GARLIC PRESS

4 (6- TO 7-INCH) PITA BREADS, WARMED

1 RIPE MEDIUM TOMATO (6 OUNCES), CUT INTO ½-INCH DICE

1 OUNCE FETA CHEESE, CRUMBLED (¼ CUP)

1 In nonstick 12-inch skillet, heat oil over medium heat until hot. Add onion and cook until tender and golden, 12 to 15 minutes, stirring occasionally. Add burger pieces, pepper, and ¼ teaspoon salt, and cook until heated through, about 5 minutes.

2 Meanwhile, in medium bowl, stir yogurt with cucumber, mint, garlic, and remaining ¼ teaspoon salt. Add burger mixture and toss gently to combine.

3 Cut 1-inch slice from each pita to make opening and reserve cut-off pita pieces for another use. Divide burger mixture evenly among pita pockets. Sprinkle with tomato and feta.

390 CALORIES **PER SANDWICH.** 24G PROTEIN | 45G CARBOHYDRATE | 13G TOTAL FAT (3G SATURATED) 6G FIBER | 9MG CHOLESTEROL | 945MG SODIUM 🟢 🌀

MAKE IT A MEAL: What could be simpler than this sandwich made from your favorite store-bought veggie burgers? Serve with Kale Chips (15 calories; page 108) for a super-wholesome 390-calorie lunch.

LASAGNA TOASTS

These open-faced sandwiches topped with fresh tomato, zucchini, basil, and cheese invite you to enjoy all the flavors of lasagna in a flash—you bake them in your toaster oven!

ACTIVE TIME: 15 MINUTES · **TOTAL TIME:** 35 MINUTES
MAKES: 4 MAIN-DISH SERVINGS

4	SLICES (½ INCH THICK) ITALIAN BREAD	⅜	TEASPOON SALT
1	MEDIUM ZUCCHINI (8 OUNCES), CUT INTO ¼-INCH CHUNKS	½	TEASPOON GROUND BLACK PEPPER
		¼	CUP PACKED FRESH BASIL LEAVES
1	GARLIC CLOVE, CRUSHED WITH GARLIC PRESS	1	CUP PART-SKIM RICOTTA CHEESE
1	TABLESPOON OLIVE OIL	¼	CUP FRESHLY GRATED PECORINO ROMANO CHEESE
4	RIPE PLUM TOMATOES (12 OUNCES), CHOPPED	4	OUNCES FRESH MOZZARELLA CHEESE, SLICED

1 Preheat toaster oven to 450°F. Toast bread 5 to 10 minutes or until golden.
2 In microwave-safe medium bowl, combine zucchini, garlic, and oil. Microwave on High for 4 minutes, stirring once. Add tomatoes and ¼ teaspoon each salt and pepper; cover with vented plastic wrap and microwave on High for 3 minutes.
3 Meanwhile, thinly slice basil leaves; reserve 2 tablespoons for garnish. In small bowl, combine basil, ricotta, Romano, and remaining ⅛ teaspoon salt and ¼ teaspoon pepper.
4 Divide ricotta mixture among bread slices and spread evenly. Using slotted spoon, divide tomato mixture among bread slices; top with mozzarella.
5 In single layer on foil-lined toaster-oven tray (working in batches if necessary), bake toasts 8 to 10 minutes or until tomato mixture is heated through and mozzarella is melted and lightly browned. Garnish with reserved basil.

320 CALORIES

PER SERVING. 18G PROTEIN | 24G CARBOHYDRATE | 17G TOTAL FAT (8G SATURATED) 3G FIBER | 46MG CHOLESTEROL | 550MG SODIUM

> **MAKE IT A MEAL:** For a quick 390-calorie lunch with Italian flair, enjoy a lasagna toast along with two of our Chocolate-Almond Meringues (35 calories each; page 138).

VEGETARIAN TACOS

Beans make a hearty stand-in for ground beef in these vegetarian tacos—especially when they're gussied up with all your favorite toppings!

ACTIVE TIME: 10 MINUTES · **TOTAL TIME:** 20 MINUTES
MAKES: 4 MAIN-DISH SERVINGS

1 TABLESPOON OLIVE OIL	2 PLUM TOMATOES, COARSELY CHOPPED
1 SMALL ONION, SLICED	¼ CUP LOOSELY PACKED FRESH CILANTRO LEAVES, CHOPPED
1 MEDIUM RED PEPPER, SLICED	
1 TEASPOON CHILI POWDER	8 (6-INCH) FLOUR TORTILLAS
¼ TEASPOON SALT	3 CUPS THINLY SLICED ROMAINE LETTUCE
1 CAN (15 TO 19 OUNCES) BLACK BEANS OR OTHER FAVORITE BEANS, RINSED AND DRAINED	2 OUNCES MONTEREY JACK OR MILD CHEDDAR CHEESE, SHREDDED (½ CUP)

1 In 12-inch nonstick skillet, heat oil over medium heat 1 minute. Add onion, pepper, chili powder, and salt; cook 10 minutes or until onion and pepper are tender, stirring occasionally. Stir in beans, tomatoes, and cilantro, and cook 3 to 4 minutes to heat through, stirring occasionally.

2 Just before serving tacos, place stack of tortillas between paper towels on microwave-safe plate; heat in microwave on High for 10 to 15 seconds to warm.

3 To serve, divide romaine lettuce and bean mixture among tortillas; top with Monterey Jack cheese, and fold over to eat out of hand.

400 CALORIES

PER SERVING. 16G PROTEIN | 61G CARBOHYDRATE | 13G TOTAL FAT (4G SATURATED) 11G FIBER | 15MG CHOLESTEROL | 840MG SODIUM ✓ ❀

MAKE IT A MEAL: You can enjoy two of these bean and veggie tacos (one serving) for lunch without further embellishment. Or finish with our Sliced Citrus with Lime Syrup (95 calories; page 140) for a zippy 495-calorie dinner.

GRILLED VEGETABLE BURRITOS

Serve these burritos with your favorite bottled salsa and a dollop of reduced-fat or nondairy sour cream, if you like.

ACTIVE TIME: 25 MINUTES · **TOTAL TIME:** 40 MINUTES
MAKES: 4 MAIN-DISH SERVINGS

4   TEASPOONS VEGETABLE OIL

1   TEASPOON CHILI POWDER

1   TEASPOON GROUND CUMIN

½   TEASPOON SALT

¼   TEASPOON COARSELY GROUND BLACK PEPPER

2   MEDIUM ZUCCHINI (8 TO 10 OUNCES EACH), CUT LENGTHWISE INTO ¼-INCH-THICK SLICES

1   LARGE ONION (12 OUNCES), CUT INTO ½-INCH-THICK SLICES

1   MEDIUM RED PEPPER, CUT INTO QUARTERS

1   MEDIUM GREEN PEPPER, CUT INTO QUARTERS

4   BURRITO-SIZED (10-INCH) FLOUR TORTILLAS

REDUCED-FAT OR NONDAIRY SOUR CREAM (OPTIONAL)

½   CUP LOOSELY PACKED FRESH CILANTRO LEAVES

BOTTLED SALSA (OPTIONAL)

1   Prepare outdoor grill for direct grilling over medium heat.

2   In small bowl, mix oil, chili powder, cumin, salt, and black pepper. Brush one side of zucchini slices, onion slices, and red and green pepper pieces with oil mixture.

3   Place vegetables, oiled side down, on hot grill rack; grill until tender and golden, 15 to 20 minutes, turning over once and transferring vegetables to plate as they are done.

4   Arrange one-fourth of grilled vegetables down center of each tortilla and dollop with sour cream, if desired. Sprinkle with cilantro, then fold sides of tortillas over filling. Serve with salsa, if you like.

330 CALORIES **PER SERVING.** 11G PROTEIN | 43G CARBOHYDRATE | 14G TOTAL FAT (4G SATURATED) 7G FIBER | 15MG CHOLESTEROL | 655MG SODIUM

MAKE IT A MEAL: For a wholesome 500-calorie dinner, pair with a simple side of Lime Couscous (170 calories; page 133).

GRILLED MEXICAN PIZZA

For an easy weeknight dinner or a backyard barbecue, this Mexican pizza recipe puts a spin on a classic dish everyone loves.

TOTAL TIME: 15 MINUTES
MAKES: 4 MAIN-DISH SERVINGS

½   CUP PREPARED BLACK BEAN DIP

1   LARGE THIN PIZZA CRUST (10 OUNCES)

½   CUP SHREDDED MEXICAN CHEESE BLEND

1   RIPE AVOCADO, CUT INTO CHUNKS

2   TABLESPOONS FRESH LIME JUICE

2   CUPS SHREDDED ROMAINE LETTUCE

¼   TEASPOON GRATED LIME PEEL

1   RIPE MEDIUM TOMATO (6 TO 8 OUNCES), CHOPPED

1   Prepare outdoor grill for covered, direct grilling over medium heat. (Or preheat oven to 450°F.)

2   Spread black bean dip evenly on crust, leaving ½-inch border; sprinkle with cheese. Place crust on hot grill rack; cover and grill until grill marks appear, 8 to 9 minutes. (Or place crust on ungreased cookie sheet. Bake 8 to 10 minutes or until cheese melts.)

3   Meanwhile, gently stir avocado with 1 tablespoon lime juice. Toss romaine with lime peel and remaining juice.

4   Top cooked pizza with romaine mixture and tomato, then with avocado. Cut into slices.

310 CALORIES   **PER SERVING.** 13G PROTEIN | 34G CARBOHYDRATE | 15G TOTAL FAT (4G SATURATED) 4G FIBER | 17MG CHOLESTEROL | 520MG SODIUM

MAKE IT A MEAL: Our pretty-in-pink Watermelon Slushie (170 calories; page 148) would make a refreshing match for this grilled pizza—and create a casual, fun 480-calorie dinner. Or pair a slice of this pizza with ten baby carrots and a dip of 2 tablespoons salsa for a 360-calorie lunch.

GRILLED WHOLE-WHEAT VEGGIE PIZZA

Everyone's favorite takeout gets a healthy makeover with a heap of veggies. You can purchase whole-wheat pizza dough, ready to roll out and bake, at some supermarkets and neighborhood pizza shops.

ACTIVE TIME: 25 MINUTES · **TOTAL TIME:** 30 MINUTES
MAKES: 4 MAIN-DISH SERVINGS

- 2 MEDIUM PORTOBELLO MUSHROOM CAPS (6 OUNCES), SLICED
- 1 SMALL RED ONION (4 TO 6 OUNCES), SLICED INTO ROUNDS
- 1 SMALL YELLOW SUMMER SQUASH, SLICED
- 1 TABLESPOON OLIVE OIL
- ¼ TEASPOON SALT
- ¼ TEASPOON PEPPER
- 1 POUND WHOLE-WHEAT PIZZA DOUGH
- 2 PLUM TOMATOES, THINLY SLICED
- ½ CUP SMOKED MOZZARELLA, SHREDDED (½ CUP)
- ¼ CUP PACKED FRESH BASIL LEAVES, SLICED

1 Prepare outdoor grill for covered direct grilling over medium heat. Brush mushrooms, onion, and squash with oil; sprinkle with salt and pepper.

2 If desired, place vegetables on grilling tray. Grill, covered, 6 minutes or until tender and browned, turning once. Separate onion rings; set aside. Reduce heat on grill to medium-low.

3 Cover large cookie sheet with foil; spray with cooking spray. Stretch dough into 10" by 14" rectangle. Place on cookie sheet.

4 Lift dough and foil; place, dough side down, on grill; gently peel off foil. Cover; cook 3 minutes or until bottom is crisp. Turn crust over. Quickly top with tomatoes, grilled vegetables, and cheese. Cover; cook 2 minutes longer or until bottom is crisp and cheese is melting. Slide onto cutting board; garnish with basil.

375 CALORIES

PER SERVING. 13G PROTEIN | 58G CARBOHYDRATE | 10G TOTAL FAT (2G SATURATED) 9G FIBER | 11MG CHOLESTEROL | 695MG SODIUM

MAKE IT A MEAL: Enjoy a slice of this pizza for a wholesome lunch or add our cooling Peachy Frozen Yogurt (130 calories; page 141) to create a yummy 505-calorie dinner.

SUMMER PHYLLO PIZZA

Using phyllo dough gives this pizza a whole different kind of crunch that you'll love. It's the perfect platform for thinly sliced sun-ripened tomatoes.

ACTIVE TIME: 15 MINUTES · **TOTAL TIME:** 35 MINUTES

MAKES: 6 MAIN-DISH SERVINGS

- 7 SHEETS (17" BY 12" EACH) FRESH OR THAWED FROZEN PHYLLO
- 5 TABLESPOONS UNSALTED BUTTER, MELTED
- 7 TABLESPOONS FRESHLY GRATED PARMESAN CHEESE
- 4 OUNCES COARSELY SHREDDED MOZZARELLA OR CRUMBLED GORGONZOLA CHEESE (1 CUP)
- 1 CUP VERY THINLY SLICED RED ONION
- 2 POUNDS RIPE TOMATOES (4 LARGE), PEELED, SEEDED, AND SLICED ¼ INCH THICK
- 1 TEASPOON FRESH THYME LEAVES OR ¼ TEASPOON DRIED, PLUS FRESH SPRIGS FOR GARNISH
- ½ TEASPOON DRIED OREGANO, CRUMBLED

1 Preheat oven to 375°F.

2 Place phyllo between two sheets waxed paper and cover with damp towel to prevent drying. Brush large cookie sheet with melted butter. Lay 1 sheet phyllo on buttered cookie sheet. Lightly brush top with butter. Sprinkle 1 tablespoon Parmesan on top of butter.

3 Place second sheet of phyllo on top and press so it adheres to first layer. Repeat brushing with butter and sprinkling with Parmesan. Continue layering phyllo sheets in same way, ending with sheet of phyllo and reserving last 1 tablespoon Parmesan.

4 Sprinkle top sheet of phyllo with mozzarella. Scatter onion evenly over cheese. Arrange tomatoes in single layer over onion. Sprinkle with thyme leaves, oregano, and remaining 1 tablespoon Parmesan.

5 Bake, making sure that phyllo browns but does not burn, 20 to 30 minutes. Garnish with thyme sprigs.

265 CALORIES · **PER SERVING.** 10G PROTEIN | 20G CARBOHYDRATE | 17G TOTAL FAT (10G SATURATED) 2G FIBER | 45MG CHOLESTEROL | 322MG SODIUM ♥

> **MAKE IT A MEAL:** For a luscious Mediterranean meal, finish with our fresh figs stuffed with ricotta, honey, and toasted almonds (170 calories; page 149). The total meal is just 435 calories—and figs are a good source of dietary fiber and potassium, so you can feel virtuous as you indulge.

BLACK BEAN BURGERS

Spicy cumin and coriander flavor these savory black bean burgers, which can be prepared in a flash in a skillet.

ACTIVE TIME: 15 MINUTES · **TOTAL TIME:** 20 MINUTES

MAKES: 4 MAIN-DISH SERVINGS

¼ CUP DRIED BREAD CRUMBS

¼ TEASPOON GROUND CUMIN

¼ TEASPOON GROUND CORIANDER

2 CANS (15 TO 19 OUNCES EACH) LOW-SODIUM BLACK BEANS, RINSED AND DRAINED

¼ CUP LIGHT MAYONNAISE

¼ TEASPOON SALT

¼ TEASPOON GROUND BLACK PEPPER

2 LARGE STALKS CELERY, FINELY CHOPPED

1 CHIPOTLE CHILE IN ADOBO (SEE TIP), FINELY CHOPPED

4 GREEN-LEAF LETTUCE LEAVES

4 WHOLE-WHEAT HAMBURGER BUNS, TOASTED

4 SLICES RIPE TOMATO

1 In food processor with knife blade attached, pulse bread crumbs, cumin, coriander, two-thirds of beans, 2 tablespoons mayonnaise, salt, and pepper until well blended. Transfer to large bowl. Stir in celery and remaining whole beans until well combined. Divide into 4 portions and shape into patties.

2 Lightly coat 12-inch nonstick skillet with nonstick cooking spray. Heat over medium heat 1 minute, then add patties. Cook 10 to 12 minutes or until browned on both sides, carefully turning once.

3 Meanwhile, in small bowl, combine chipotle chile and remaining 2 tablespoons mayonnaise until well mixed. Place 1 lettuce leaf on bottom of each bun; top with patty, then tomato slice. Divide chipotle mayonnaise among burgers and replace tops of buns to serve.

TIP Chipotle chiles in adobo are dried, smoked jalapeño chiles canned in a thick puree. They are found in many supermarkets and Latin-American markets.

 370 CALORIES **PER SERVING.** 18G PROTEIN | 59G CARBOHYDRATE | 8G TOTAL FAT (1G SATURATED) 14G FIBER | 5MG CHOLESTEROL | 725MG SODIUM

MAKE IT A MEAL: Make these Black Bean Burgers a 500-calorie dinner by adding our Wheat-Berry Salad with Dried Cherries (130 calories; page 126), and you'll get your grains along with your beans!

PORTOBELLO PESTO BURGERS

These hearty portobello burgers, topped with pesto and a carrot-fennel slaw, are satisfying and easy to prepare in the toaster oven (or traditional oven). For photo, see page 18.

ACTIVE TIME: 20 MINUTES · **TOTAL TIME:** 45 MINUTES
MAKES: 4 BURGERS

CARROT-FENNEL SLAW

2   CUPS SHREDDED CARROTS

1   SMALL FENNEL BULB (6 OUNCES), TRIMMED AND THINLY SLICED

½   CUP LOOSELY PACKED FRESH BASIL LEAVES, THINLY SLICED

2   TEASPOONS OLIVE OIL

1½ TEASPOONS CIDER VINEGAR

¼   TEASPOON SALT

¼   TEASPOON GROUND BLACK PEPPER

PORTOBELLO BURGERS

4   PORTOBELLO MUSHROOMS (1 POUND)

¼   CUP PREPARED SUN-DRIED-TOMATO PESTO

4   WHOLE-GRAIN HAMBURGER BUNS, SPLIT

1   LARGE RIPE TOMATO (10 TO 12 OUNCES), CUT INTO 8 SLICES

1   LOG (4 OUNCES) FRESH GOAT CHEESE, CUT CROSSWISE INTO 8 SLICES

8   LARGE FRESH BASIL LEAVES

1 Prepare slaw: In large bowl, mix carrots, fennel, basil, oil, vinegar, salt, and pepper until well combined. Set aside.

2 Prepare burgers: Preheat toaster oven to 425°F. Place portobellos on foil-lined toaster oven tray, rounded side up. Bake 14 minutes; turn mushrooms over and spread 1 tablespoon pesto evenly on each. Bake 10 minutes or until mushrooms are just tender.

3 Toast buns. Place 2 tomato slices on bottom of each bun. Top each with 1 portobello, 2 slices goat cheese, 2 basil leaves, and top of bun. Serve with Carrot-Fennel Slaw.

345 CALORIES **PER BURGER.** 15G PROTEIN | 38G CARBOHYDRATE | 16G TOTAL FAT (6G SATURATED) 8G FIBER | 13MG CHOLESTEROL | 635MG SODIUM 🌱

MAKE IT A MEAL: These easy portobello burgers will freshen up your lunch-time routine. Add a quick side of our Sun-Dried Tomato and Green Onion Couscous (180 calories; page 133) for a 525-calorie dinner.

BARBECUED TOFU SANDWICHES

Here's a quick and easy way to flavor tofu.

ACTIVE TIME: 20 MINUTES · **TOTAL TIME:** 25 MINUTES PLUS DRAINING TOFU
MAKES: 4 SANDWICHES

¼ CUP KETCHUP

2 TABLESPOONS DIJON MUSTARD

2 TABLESPOONS REDUCED-SODIUM SOY SAUCE

1 TABLESPOON MOLASSES

1 TABLESPOON GRATED, PEELED FRESH GINGER

⅛ TEASPOON CAYENNE (GROUND RED) PEPPER

2 GARLIC CLOVES, CRUSHED WITH GARLIC PRESS

1 PACKAGE (16 OUNCES) EXTRA-FIRM TOFU, DRAINED AND PRESSED (SEE PAGE 15)

2 TEASPOONS SESAME SEEDS

8 SLICES WHOLE-GRAIN BREAD, TOASTED

SLICED RIPE TOMATOES, SLICED RED ONION, AND LETTUCE LEAVES (OPTIONAL)

1 Preheat broiler. Coat rack in broiling pan with nonstick cooking spray.
2 In small bowl, combine ketchup, mustard, soy sauce, molasses, ginger, cayenne, and garlic, stirring until blended.
3 Cut tofu lengthwise into 8 slices.
4 Place slices on rack in broiling pan; brush with half of ketchup mixture. Place in broiler about 5 inches from source of heat and broil tofu until ketchup mixture looks dry, about 3 minutes. With metal spatula, turn slices over; brush with remaining ketchup mixture and sprinkle with sesame seeds. Broil tofu 3 minutes longer.
5 To serve, place 2 tofu slices on 1 slice toasted bread. Top with tomato, onion, and lettuce, if you like. Top with another slice of bread. Repeat with remaining tofu and bread to make remaining sandwiches.

230 CALORIES

PER SANDWICH. 14G PROTEIN | 35G CARBOHYDRATE | 5G TOTAL FAT (0G SATURATED) 2G FIBER | 0MG CHOLESTEROL | 975MG SODIUM Ⓥ ⊛

MAKE IT A MEAL: For a filling 380-calorie lunch, pair this quick vegetarian barbecue with our Healthy Makeover Potato Salad (150 calories; page 120).

205
CALORIES
Ginger Carrot Soup
(page 41)

SOUPS & STEWS

Beans and other legumes are an important part of the vegetarian diet, and the soup pot is where they really shine. Here you'll find a soul-satisfying selection of bean and lentil recipes made special with an exciting array of international flavors: Try a warming bowl of our Latin-style Black Bean Soup or our hearty chili recipe. Soup is also an easy, satisfying way to make sure you eat your vegetables: Enjoy our cooling Gazpacho with Cilantro Cream or our cozy Winter Vegetable Chowder. Want to get better acquainted with tofu? Our Hot and Sour Soup with Tofu is simple to make and tastier than Chinese takeout.

KEY TO ICONS

⊘ 30 minutes or less   Ⓥ Vegan   ♥ Heart healthy   ⊛ High fiber   ▭ Make ahead

RED LENTIL AND VEGETABLE SOUP

This meal-in-a-bowl brims with filling soluble fiber, thanks to the lentils. Translation: It may help keep weight down and also lower total and "bad" LDL cholesterol. The lentils, spinach, and tomatoes, all rich in potassium, work to keep blood pressure in check, too.

ACTIVE TIME: 20 MINUTES · **TOTAL TIME:** 30 MINUTES
MAKES: 4 MAIN-DISH SERVINGS

1 TABLESPOON OLIVE OIL	1 CAN (14½ OUNCES) VEGETABLE BROTH OR 13¾ CUPS HOMEMADE BROTH (OPPOSITE)
4 MEDIUM CARROTS, PEELED AND CHOPPED	2 CUPS WATER
1 SMALL ONION, CHOPPED	¼ TEASPOON SALT
1 TEASPOON GROUND CUMIN	⅛ TEASPOON GROUND BLACK PEPPER
1 CAN (14½ OUNCES) DICED TOMATOES	1 BAG (5 OUNCES) BABY SPINACH
1 CUP RED LENTILS, RINSED AND PICKED THROUGH	

1 In 4-quart saucepan, heat oil over medium heat until hot. Add carrots and onion, and cook until tender and lightly browned, 6 to 8 minutes. Stir in cumin; cook 1 minute.

2 Add tomatoes with their juice, lentils, broth, water, salt, and pepper; cover and heat to boiling over high heat. Reduce heat to low; cover and simmer until lentils are tender, 8 to 10 minutes.

3 Just before serving, stir in spinach.

265 CALORIES **PER SERVING.** 16G PROTEIN | 41G CARBOHYDRATE | 5G TOTAL FAT (1G SATURATED) 13G FIBER | 0MG CHOLESTEROL | 645MG SODIUM ☺ Ⓥ ✿ 📦

MAKE IT A MEAL: One of our easy Whole-Wheat Sesame Biscuits (125 calories; page 125) is all you need to turn this soup into a wholesome 390-calorie lunch.

HOMEMADE VEGETABLE BROTH

It's great in soups, risottos, and sauces. The optional fennel and parsnip lend a natural sweetness and additional depth of flavor.

ACTIVE TIME: 25 MINUTES · **TOTAL TIME:** 2 HOURS 25 MINUTES
MAKES: ABOUT 6 CUPS

4 LARGE LEEKS

2 TO 4 GARLIC CLOVES, NOT PEELED

13 CUPS WATER

SALT

1 LARGE ALL-PURPOSE POTATO, PEELED, CUT LENGTHWISE IN HALF, AND THINLY SLICED

1 SMALL FENNEL BULB (6 OUNCES), TRIMMED AND CHOPPED (OPTIONAL)

3 PARSNIPS, PEELED AND THINLY SLICED (OPTIONAL)

2 LARGE CARROTS, PEELED AND THINLY SLICED

3 STALKS CELERY WITH LEAVES, THINLY SLICED

4 OUNCES MUSHROOMS, TRIMMED AND THINLY SLICED

10 PARSLEY SPRIGS

4 THYME SPRIGS

2 BAY LEAVES

1 TEASPOON WHOLE BLACK PEPPERCORNS

1 Trim and discard roots and dark green tops from leeks; thinly slice leeks. Rinse leeks in large bowl of cold water, swishing to remove sand. Lift out and place in colander, leaving sand in bowl.

2 In 6-quart saucepot, combine leeks, garlic, 1 cup water, and pinch salt; heat to boiling. Reduce heat to medium; cover and cook until leeks are tender, about 15 minutes.

3 Add potato, fennel if using, parsnips if using, carrots, celery, mushrooms, parsley and thyme sprigs, bay leaves, peppercorns, and remaining 12 cups water. Heat to boiling; reduce heat and simmer, uncovered, at least 1 hour 30 minutes.

4 Taste and continue cooking if flavor is not concentrated enough. Season with salt and pepper to taste. Strain broth through fine-mesh sieve into containers, pressing on solids with back of wooden spoon; cool. Cover and refrigerate to up to 3 days, or freeze up to 4 months.

20 CALORIES

PER CUP. 1G PROTEIN | 4G CARBOHYDRATE | 0G TOTAL FAT (0G SATURATED) 0MG CHOLESTEROL | 0G FIBER | 9MG SODIUM

GAZPACHO WITH CILANTRO CREAM

Recipes for gazpacho abound. This version is topped with a dollop of cilantro-spiked sour cream, a tasty combination.

TOTAL TIME: 30 MINUTES PLUS CHILLING

MAKES: 6 MAIN-DISH SERVINGS

4   MEDIUM CUCUMBERS (8 OUNCES EACH), PEELED

2   MEDIUM YELLOW PEPPERS (4 TO 6 OUNCES EACH)

4   POUNDS RIPE TOMATOES, PEELED, SEEDED, AND CHOPPED

1   TO 2 SMALL JALAPEÑO CHILES, SEEDED (TO TASTE)

6   TABLESPOONS FRESH LIME JUICE

¼   CUP EXTRA-VIRGIN OLIVE OIL

1¾ TEASPOONS SALT

½   SMALL RED ONION, COARSELY CHOPPED

½   CUP REDUCED-FAT SOUR CREAM OR PLAIN LOW-FAT YOGURT

2   TABLESPOONS MILK

2   TABLESPOONS PLUS 2 TEASPOONS CHOPPED FRESH CILANTRO

1   Coarsely chop 1 cucumber and 1 yellow pepper; set aside. Cut remaining cucumbers and yellow pepper into large pieces for pureeing.

2   In blender or food processor with knife blade attached, puree large pieces of cucumber and yellow pepper, tomatoes, jalapeño, lime juice, oil, and 1½ teaspoons salt until smooth. Pour puree into bowl; add coarsely chopped cucumber, yellow pepper, and onion. Cover and refrigerate until well chilled, at least 6 hours and up to overnight.

3   In small bowl, stir sour cream, milk, cilantro, and remaining ¼ teaspoon salt until smooth. Cover and refrigerate.

4   To serve, top soup with dollops of cilantro cream.

210 CALORIES

PER SERVING. 5G PROTEIN | 23G CARBOHYDRATE | 13G TOTAL FAT (3G SATURATED) 5G FIBER | 8MG CHOLESTEROL | 727MG SODIUM

MAKE IT A MEAL: To create a summery 400-calorie lunch, pair this fresh and colorful soup with a salad of crisp greens and ½ cup cubed avocado; for dessert, have an orange (190 calories for salad and orange).

BLACK BEAN SOUP

This simple but hearty soup is sure to become a standby. The cilantro and fresh lime juice add Latin flavor.

ACTIVE TIME: 15 MINUTES · **TOTAL TIME:** 45 MINUTES PLUS COOLING
MAKES: 6½ CUPS OR 6 MAIN-DISH SERVINGS

1	TABLESPOON OLIVE OIL	½	TEASPOON SALT
2	MEDIUM CARROTS, PEELED AND CHOPPED	2	CUPS WATER
2	GARLIC CLOVES, FINELY CHOPPED	2	CANS BLACK BEANS (15 TO 19 OUNCES EACH), RINSED AND DRAINED
1	LARGE ONION (12 OUNCES), CHOPPED	1	CAN (14½ OUNCES) VEGETABLE BROTH OR 1¾ CUPS HOMEMADE BROTH (PAGE 37)
1	MEDIUM RED PEPPER (4 TO 6 OUNCES), CHOPPED		
2	TEASPOONS GROUND CUMIN	¼	CUP FRESH CILANTRO LEAVES, CHOPPED, PLUS SPRIGS FOR GARNISH
¼	TEASPOON CRUSHED RED PEPPER	1	TABLESPOON FRESH LIME JUICE

1 In 6-quart saucepot, heat oil over medium heat until hot. Add carrots, garlic, onion, and pepper; cook 12 to 15 minutes or until vegetables are lightly browned and tender, stirring occasionally. Add cumin, crushed red pepper, and salt; cook 1 minute.

2 Stir in water, beans, and broth; heat to boiling over medium-high heat. Reduce heat to low and simmer, uncovered, 15 minutes to blend flavors.

3 Ladle 3 cups soup into blender; remove center part of lid to allow steam to escape, cover soup, and blend until pureed. Stir puree into soup in saucepot; heat through over medium heat. Stir in cilantro and lime juice. Serve garnished with cilantro sprigs.

250 CALORIES **PER SERVING.** 14G PROTEIN | 50G CARBOHYDRATE | 5G TOTAL FAT (0G SATURATED) 17G FIBER | 0MG CHOLESTEROL | 1,058MG SODIUM

MAKE IT A MEAL: For a 350-calorie lunch, add on half a mini pita stuffed with 2 tablespoons each mashed avocado and chopped tomato. For a 500-calorie dinner, finish this Latin-inspired meal with our Broiled Brown-Sugar Bananas (150 calories; page 144).

GINGER CARROT SOUP

This creamy-smooth soup is supercharged with vision-enhancing vitamin A. Subbing ginger-steeped green tea for stock slashes sodium. For photo, see page 34.

ACTIVE TIME: 25 MINUTES · **TOTAL TIME:** 55 MINUTES
MAKES: 4 MAIN-DISH SERVINGS

4   GREEN ONIONS

1   (1-INCH) PIECE FRESH GINGER

5   CUPS WATER

3   TEA BAGS GREEN TEA

1   TABLESPOON OLIVE OIL

1   MEDIUM ONION, FINELY CHOPPED

1½ POUNDS CARROTS, PEELED AND CUT INTO ¾-INCH-THICK PIECES

1   MEDIUM ALL-PURPOSE POTATO, PEELED AND CHOPPED

½   TEASPOON SALT

¼   TEASPOON GROUND BLACK PEPPER

2   CUPS FROZEN PEAS

1   From green onions, cut off white and pale green parts and place in 5-quart saucepot. Thinly slice dark green onion parts; set aside. From ginger, cut 4 slices; set aside. Peel remaining piece of ginger and grate enough to make 1 teaspoon; set aside.

2   To saucepot, add sliced ginger and water. Heat to boiling over high heat. Add tea bags. Cover, remove from heat, and let stand 10 minutes.

3   While tea steeps, in 12-inch skillet, heat oil over medium-high heat. Add onion, carrots, potato, and ¼ teaspoon each salt and pepper. Cook, stirring, 6 minutes or until golden. Add grated ginger; cook 1 minute, stirring.

4   With slotted spoon, remove ginger, tea bags, and green onion pieces from pot and discard after squeezing excess liquid back into pot. Heat ginger tea to boiling over high heat; stir in carrot mixture. Reduce heat to maintain simmer. Cook 10 minutes or until vegetables are tender, stirring.

5   Transfer half of soup to blender; keep remaining soup simmering. Carefully puree until smooth, then return to pot. Stir in peas and remaining ¼ teaspoon salt. Cook 3 minutes or until peas are bright green and hot. Divide among soup bowls; garnish with sliced green onions.

205 CALORIES

PER SERVING. 7G PROTEIN | 37G CARBOHYDRATE | 4G TOTAL FAT (1G SATURATED) 9G FIBER | 0MG CHOLESTEROL | 410MG SODIUM ♥ ♥ ♥

MAKE IT A MEAL: For a nutrient-dense 365-calorie lunch, add on our Chunky Vegetable Bulgar Salad (160 calories; page 131) to throw some grains and legumes into the mix.

NOT YOUR GRANDMA'S VEGETABLE SOUP

It's impossible to peel beets without getting red all over your hands—unless you wear rubber gloves. For extra-easy cleanup, peel beets in the sink, too.

ACTIVE TIME: 15 MINUTES · **TOTAL TIME:** 1 HOUR 15 MINUTES
MAKES: 5 MAIN-DISH SERVINGS

1   TABLESPOON OLIVE OIL

1   ONION, CHOPPED

1   GARLIC CLOVE, CRUSHED WITH GARLIC PRESS

½   TEASPOON GROUND ALLSPICE

1   CAN (14½ OUNCES) DICED TOMATOES

1   POUND BEETS (NOT INCLUDING TOPS)

6   CUPS SLICED GREEN CABBAGE (1 POUND)

3   LARGE CARROTS, PEELED AND CUT INTO ½-INCH CHUNKS

4   CUPS WATER

1   CAN (14½ OUNCES) VEGETABLE BROTH OR 1¾ CUPS HOMEMADE BROTH (PAGE 37)

1   BAY LEAF

¾   TEASPOON SALT

2   TABLESPOONS RED WINE VINEGAR

¼   CUP LOOSELY PACKED FRESH DILL OR PARSLEY LEAVES, CHOPPED

REDUCED-FAT OR NONDAIRY SOUR CREAM (OPTIONAL)

1   In 5- to 6-quart saucepot, heat oil over medium heat until hot. Add onion and cook until tender, about 8 minutes. Stir in garlic and allspice; cook 30 seconds. Add tomatoes with their juice and cook 5 minutes.

2   Meanwhile, peel beets and shred in food processor (or using coarse side of box grater).

3   Add beets to onion mixture along with cabbage, carrots, water, broth, bay leaf, and salt; heat to boiling over high heat. Reduce heat to medium-low; cover and simmer until all vegetables are tender, about 30 minutes.

4   Remove bay leaf. Stir in vinegar and dill. Serve soup with sour cream, if you like.

200 CALORIES **PER SERVING.** 6G PROTEIN | 34G CARBOHYDRATE | 6G TOTAL FAT (1G SATURATED) 6G FIBER | 6MG CHOLESTEROL | 1,150MG SODIUM

MAKE IT A MEAL: Add creamy satisfaction with 1 tablespoon reduced-fat or nondairy sour cream (20 calories). Finish with warm Apple-Oat Crisp (175 calories; page 149) and you have a 395-calorie lunch.

WINTER VEGETABLE CHOWDER

We developed this slow-cooker recipe with leftovers in mind. Freeze any extra for a weekday meal that is ready whenever you are!

ACTIVE TIME: 40 MINUTES · **TOTAL TIME:** 1 HOUR 15 MINUTES
MAKES: 8 MAIN-DISH SERVINGS

6	MEDIUM LEEKS, TRIMMED	4	CUPS WATER
2	TABLESPOONS OLIVE OIL	½	TEASPOON CHOPPED FRESH THYME PLUS WHOLE SPRIGS FOR GARNISH
4	STALKS CELERY, CHOPPED		
3	MEDIUM PARSNIPS, PEELED AND CHOPPED	1	TEASPOON SALT
2	MEDIUM RED POTATOES, CUT INTO ½-INCH PIECES	¾	TEASPOON COARSELY GROUND BLACK PEPPER
2	POUNDS BUTTERNUT SQUASH, PEELED, SEEDED, AND CUT INTO ½-INCH PIECES	1	CUP HALF-AND-HALF OR LIGHT CREAM
2	CANS (14½ OUNCES EACH) VEGETABLE BROTH OR 3½ CUPS HOMEMADE BROTH (PAGE 37)		

1 Trim and discard roots and dark-green tops from leeks. Discard any tough outer leaves. Cut each leek lengthwise in half, then crosswise into ½-inch-thick slices. Rinse in large bowl of cold water; swish to remove sand. With hands, transfer leeks to colander, leaving sand in bottom of bowl. Repeat rinsing and draining several times, until all sand is removed. Drain well.
2 In 6-quart saucepot, heat oil over medium-high heat until hot. Add leeks, celery, and parsnips, and cook until all vegetables are tender, 10 to 12 minutes, stirring occasionally.
3 Add potatoes, squash, broth, water, chopped thyme, salt, and pepper; heat to boiling over medium-high heat. Reduce heat to medium-low; cover and simmer until potatoes and squash are tender, about 10 minutes.
4 Stir in half-and-half and heat through, about 13 minutes. Spoon soup into tureen and garnish with thyme sprigs.

5 To store leftovers, spoon soup into freezer-safe containers and freeze. Before serving, thaw overnight in refrigerator or follow manufacturer instructions for thawing in microwave. To heat thawed soup on stovetop, pour into saucepan, cover, and heat to boiling over medium, about 25 minutes, stirring often. To use microwave, pour into microwave-safe bowl, cover, and heat on Low (30 percent) 10 minutes, stirring once or twice, then on High for 15 to 20 minutes, stirring once.

215 CALORIES

PER SERVING. 5G PROTEIN | 35G CARBOHYDRATE | 8G TOTAL FAT (3G SATURATED) 5G FIBER | 11MG CHOLESTEROL | 560MG SODIUM 🌱 🍽

MAKE IT A MEAL: Serve this chowder with a fresh-from-the-oven popover (160 calories; page 132) and you'll have a thoroughly satisfying 375-calorie lunch. You can make the popovers ahead and reheat in a 400°F oven for 15 minutes.

RED CHILI WITH FIRE-ROASTED TOMATOES

Beets, chipotle chili powder, and fire-roasted tomatoes give this chili a beautiful color—it would be perfect for Valentine's Day.

ACTIVE TIME: 35 MINUTES · **TOTAL TIME:** 1 HOUR 30 MINUTES
MAKES: 9 CUPS OR 6 MAIN-DISH SERVINGS

2 TEASPOONS GROUND CUMIN	1 CAN (28 OUNCES) FIRE-ROASTED DICED TOMATOES
1 TEASPOON DRIED OREGANO	
½ TEASPOON CHIPOTLE CHILE POWDER	1 CAN (15 TO 19 OUNCES) LOW-SODIUM BLACK BEANS, RINSED AND DRAINED
2 TABLESPOONS VEGETABLE OIL	1 CAN (15 TO 19 OUNCES) LOW-SODIUM RED KIDNEY BEANS, RINSED AND DRAINED
3 LARGE BEETS (6 TO 8 OUNCES EACH) , TRIMMED, PEELED, AND CHOPPED	
1 JUMBO RED ONION (1 POUND), FINELY CHOPPED	1 CAN (15 TO 19 OUNCES) LOW-SODIUM PINTO BEANS, RINSED AND DRAINED
1 LARGE RED PEPPER (8 TO 10 OUNCES), CHOPPED	1 CUP WATER
½ TEASPOON GROUND BLACK PEPPER	1 CUP REDUCED-FAT SOUR CREAM
4 GARLIC CLOVES, CRUSHED WITH GARLIC PRESS	¼ CUP FRESH CILANTRO LEAVES

1 In 7- to 8-quart Dutch oven or heavy saucepot, combine cumin, oregano, and chipotle powder. Cook over medium heat 1 to 2 minutes or until toasted and fragrant. Transfer to sheet of waxed paper; set aside. In same Dutch oven, heat oil over medium heat until hot. Add beets, onion, pepper, and ¼ teaspoon black pepper. Cook 15 minutes or until vegetables are tender, stirring occasionally.

2 Add garlic and reserved spice mixture. Cook 2 minutes, stirring constantly. Add tomatoes, all beans, and water. Heat to boiling over medium-high heat. Reduce heat to medium-low and simmer 30 minutes, stirring and mashing some beans occasionally. Season with remaining ¼ teaspoon black pepper. (Can be prepared up to this point up to 2 days ahead; transfer to airtight container and refrigerate. Reheat before serving.) Divide among serving bowls and top with sour cream and cilantro.

345
CALORIES

PER SERVING. 18G PROTEIN | 59G CARBOHYDRATE | 8G TOTAL FAT (1G SATURATED) 14G FIBER | 5MG CHOLESTEROL | 725MG SODIUM

MAKE IT A MEAL: For a hearty weeknight meal or casual dinner with friends, add our Double Cornbread (125 calories; page 124) and Sautéed Spinach with Garlic and Lemon (45 calories; page 109). You can enjoy it all for 515 calories per serving.

CAULIFLOWER-CURRY STEW

This easy-to-make vegetarian stew owes its complex flavor to spicy, fresh ginger and traditional Indian curry powder.

ACTIVE TIME: 25 MINUTES · **TOTAL TIME:** 50 MINUTES

MAKES: 8 MAIN-DISH SERVINGS

---

1 TABLESPOON OLIVE OIL

3 CARROTS, PEELED AND CHOPPED

1 ONION, CHOPPED

1½ CUPS BROWN RICE

1 TABLESPOON FINELY CHOPPED, PEELED FRESH GINGER

1 TABLESPOON CURRY POWDER

¾ TEASPOON SALT

2½ CUPS CANNED OR HOMEMADE VEGETABLE BROTH (PAGE 37)

1 MEDIUM (2-POUND) HEAD CAULIFLOWER, CUT INTO SMALL FLOWERETS

2 CANS (15 TO 19 OUNCES EACH) GARBANZO BEANS (CHICKPEAS), RINSED AND DRAINED

½ CUP LOOSELY PACKED FRESH CILANTRO LEAVES, CHOPPED

¼ CUP PLAIN LOW-FAT YOGURT PLUS ADDITIONAL FOR SERVING

---

1 In 6-quart Dutch oven, heat oil over medium-high heat until hot. Add carrots and onion, and cook 10 to 12 minutes or until vegetables are lightly browned and tender, stirring frequently.

2 Meanwhile, prepare rice as label directs; keep warm.

3 Stir ginger, curry, and salt into carrot mixture; cook 3 minutes, stirring constantly. Add broth; cover and heat to boiling on high. Stir in cauliflower and garbanzo beans; cover and cook over medium heat 15 to 20 minutes longer, gently stirring every 5 minutes until cauliflower is tender.

4 To serve, stir chopped cilantro and ¼ cup yogurt into cauliflower stew. Spoon rice into serving bowls; top with stew. Serve cauliflower stew with additional yogurt to dollop on top.

---

360 CALORIES

PER SERVING. 12G PROTEIN | 68G CARBOHYDRATE | 5G TOTAL FAT (1G SATURATED) 10G FIBER | 1MG CHOLESTEROL | 650MG SODIUM 🌱 🍲

MAKE IT A MEAL: Turn this stew into a hearty 460-calorie dinner: Start with one Ak-Mak Stone Ground Whole Wheat Cracker spread with 1 tablespoon mashed avocado (45 calories) and serve a side salad of Shredded Beets with Celery and Dates (50 calories; page 110).

HOT AND SOUR TOFU SOUP

We streamlined seasonings to help get this popular Asian soup on the table in record time—without sacrificing the great taste.

ACTIVE TIME: 15 MINUTES · **TOTAL TIME:** 30 MINUTES PLUS DRAINING TOFU
MAKES: 4 MAIN-DISH SERVINGS

- 1 TABLESPOON VEGETABLE OIL
- 4 OUNCES SHIITAKE MUSHROOMS, STEMS DISCARDED AND CAPS THINLY SLICED
- 3 TABLESPOONS REDUCED-SODIUM SOY SAUCE
- 1 PACKAGE (16 OUNCES) EXTRA-FIRM TOFU, DRAINED AND PRESSED (SEE PAGE 15), CUT INTO 1-INCH CUBES
- 2 TABLESPOONS CORNSTARCH
- 1 CUP WATER
- 1 CARTON (32 OUNCES) VEGETABLE BROTH OR 4 CUPS HOMEMADE BROTH (PAGE 37)

- 3 TABLESPOONS SEASONED RICE VINEGAR
- 2 TABLESPOONS GRATED, PEELED FRESH GINGER
- 1 TABLESPOON WORCESTERSHIRE SAUCE
- ½ TEASPOON ASIAN SESAME OIL
- ¼ TEASPOON CAYENNE (GROUND RED) PEPPER
- 2 LARGE EGGS, BEATEN
- 2 GREEN ONIONS, THINLY SLICED

1 In nonstick 5-quart saucepot, heat vegetable oil over medium-high heat until hot. Add mushrooms, soy sauce, and tofu, and cook until liquid evaporates, about 5 minutes, gently stirring often.

2 In cup, with fork, mix cornstarch with ¼ cup water until cornstarch is dissolved; set aside. Add broth and remaining ¾ cup water to tofu mixture; heat to boiling over high heat. Stir in cornstarch mixture and boil 30 seconds, stirring. Reduce heat to medium-low; stir in vinegar, ginger, Worcestershire, sesame oil, and cayenne, and simmer 5 minutes.

3 Remove saucepot from heat. Slowly pour beaten eggs into soup in a thin, steady stream around the edge of the saucepot. Carefully stir the soup once so eggs separate into strands. Serve sprinkled with green onions.

280 CALORIES **PER SERVING.** 18G PROTEIN | 17G CARBOHYDRATE | 15G TOTAL FAT (3G SATURATED) 1G FIBER | 106MG CHOLESTEROL | 1,790MG SODIUM

MAKE IT A MEAL: Skip the Chinese takeout and serve this soup with ¾ cup basmati rice (150 calories) topped with our tasty Vegetables with Sesame Vinaigrette (80 calories; page 111) for an easy 510-calorie supper.

MOROCCAN SWEET POTATO STEW

With just 2 teaspoons of olive oil, this fragrant stew is both heart-healthy and satisfying.

ACTIVE TIME: 15 MINUTES · **TOTAL TIME:** 45 MINUTES

MAKES: 4 MAIN-DISH SERVINGS

2   TEASPOONS OLIVE OIL

1   MEDIUM YELLOW ONION, CHOPPED

3   GARLIC CLOVES, CRUSHED
    WITH GARLIC PRESS

1½ TEASPOONS CURRY POWDER

1½ TEASPOONS GROUND CUMIN

¼   TEASPOON GROUND ALLSPICE

1   CAN (14½ OUNCES) DICED TOMATOES

1   CAN (14½ OUNCES) REDUCED-SODIUM
    VEGETABLE BROTH OR 1¾ CUPS
    HOMEMADE BROTH (PAGE 37)

1   CUP NO-SALT-ADDED GARBANZO
    BEANS, RINSED AND DRAINED

1   LARGE SWEET POTATO (1 POUND),
    PEELED AND CUT INTO ¾-INCH CHUNKS

2   SMALL ZUCCHINI (6 OUNCES EACH),
    CUT INTO ¾-INCH CHUNKS

1   CUP WHOLE-GRAIN COUSCOUS
    (MOROCCAN PASTA)

¼   CUP LOOSELY PACKED FRESH
    MINT LEAVES, CHOPPED

1   In nonstick 12-inch skillet, heat oil over medium heat until hot. Add onion and cook until tender and lightly browned, 8 to 10 minutes, stirring occasionally. Stir in garlic, curry powder, cumin, and allspice; cook 30 seconds.

2   Add tomatoes and their juices, broth, beans, and sweet potato; cover and heat to boiling over medium-high heat. Reduce heat to medium and cook 10 minutes.

3   Stir in zucchini, cover, and cook until vegetables are tender, about 10 minutes. Meanwhile, prepare couscous as label directs.

4   Stir mint into stew. Serve stew with couscous.

360 CALORIES

PER SERVING. 14G PROTEIN | 70G CARBOHYDRATE | 5G TOTAL FAT (1G SATURATED) 13G FIBER | 0MG CHOLESTEROL | 670MG SODIUM ⓥ ⓧ ⌷

MAKE IT A MEAL: For authentic flavor, swap in our Moroccan-flavored couscous (adds 35 calories; page 133) and add a side of iron-rich Kale Chips (15 calories; page 108). You'll have a colorful, nutrient-dense meal for just 410 calories per serving.

**260
CALORIES**

*Green Tomato Stacks
(page 54)*

STUFFED, STACKED & STIR-FRIED

If you've been preparing vegetarian meals, you've probably steamed, sautéed, and roasted vegetables. But have you tried stuffing or stacking them? Here we offer lots of tempting recipes that do just that. Stuff chile peppers, artichokes, or acorn squash with veggies, whole grains, and seasonings to create satisfying vegetarian mains that are as wholesome as they are fun to eat. Or layer bread-crumb-crusted fried green tomatoes and top the stack with a luscious lemony chive and mayonnaise sauce. Tossing your veggies is a third quick and playful option: Check out the Fast Fried Rice and lo mein and our clever Sweet-and-Sour Unstuffed Cabbage.

KEY TO ICONS

🕑 30 minutes or less   Ⓥ Vegan   ♥ Heart healthy   🌾 High fiber   🍱 Make ahead

GREEN TOMATO STACKS

Fried green tomatoes make a luscious summer meal. We top ours with chive-and-lemon-spiked mayo. Delish! For photo, see page 52.

TOTAL TIME: 25 MINUTES

MAKES: 4 MAIN-DISH SERVINGS

---

1 LARGE EGG WHITE	2 RIPE MEDIUM RED TOMATOES (6 TO 8 OUNCES EACH
⅓ CUP CORNMEAL	
½ TEASPOON COARSELY GROUND BLACK PEPPER	3 TABLESPOONS OLIVE OIL
	1 LEMON
¼ TEASPOON SALT	⅓ CUP LIGHT MAYONNAISE
2 MEDIUM GREEN TOMATOES (6 TO 8 OUNCES EACH)	2 TABLESPOONS SNIPPED FRESH CHIVES
	8 SLICES MEATLESS CANADIAN BACON (SUCH AS YVES BRAND; OPTIONAL)

1 In pie plate, with fork, beat egg white. On waxed paper, mix cornmeal and ¼ teaspoon pepper. Cut each tomato into 4 slices and sprinkle with salt. Dip green tomato slices in egg white, then into cornmeal mixture to coat both sides. Place on waxed paper.

2 In 12-inch skillet, heat half of oil over medium-high heat until hot. Add 2 green tomato slices, and cook 4 to 5 minutes or until golden-brown on both sides and heated through, turning over once and reducing heat to medium if tomatoes brown too quickly. Transfer tomatoes to plate. Repeat with remaining oil and green tomato slices.

3 Meanwhile, from lemon, grate 1 teaspoon peel and squeeze 2 table-spoons juice. In small bowl, mix lemon peel and juice with mayonnaise, chives, and remaining ¼ teaspoon pepper; set aside.

4 If using meatless bacon, add to same skillet and cook over medium-high heat 2 to 3 minutes or until lightly browned on both sides and heated through, turning slices over once. Cut slices in half.

5 To serve, on each dinner plate, alternately stack slices of red tomato and fried green tomatoes and bacon; drizzle with lemon-chive mayonnaise.

---

285 CALORIES

PER SERVING. 15G PROTEIN | 22G CARBOHYDRATE | 16G TOTAL FAT (2G SATURATED) 3G FIBER | 7MG CHOLESTEROL | 654MG SODIUM ☺

> **MAKE IT A MEAL:** Pair these with Millet with Corn and Green Chiles (150 calories; page 129) and finish with 1 cup cubed watermelon (45 calories). A light and refreshing dinner for just 480 calories per serving.

STUFFED ACORN SQUASH

Preparation of this dish is easy and efficient, because the beans cook on the stovetop while the squash steams in the microwave.

ACTIVE TIME: 30 MINUTES · **TOTAL TIME:** 35 MINUTES

MAKES: 4 MAIN-DISH SERVINGS

1 TABLESPOON OLIVE OIL	¼ TEASPOON SALT
1 JUMBO ONION (1 POUND), CUT INTO ¼-INCH DICE	¼ TEASPOON COARSELY GROUND BLACK PEPPER
1 MEDIUM CARROT, PEELED AND CUT INTO ¼-INCH DICE	1 TABLESPOON CHOPPED FRESH SAGE PLUS SAGE SPRIGS FOR GARNISH
2 GARLIC CLOVES, CRUSHED WITH GARLIC PRESS	2 VERY SMALL ACORN SQUASHES (12 OUNCES EACH)
1 CAN (15 TO 19 OUNCES) WHITE KIDNEY BEANS (CANNELLINI), RINSED AND DRAINED	1 RIPE MEDIUM TOMATO (6 TO 8 OUNCES), CUT INTO ¼-INCH DICE
¾ CUP CANNED OR HOMEMADE VEGETABLE BROTH (PAGE 37)	FRESHLY GRATED PARMESAN CHEESE (OPTIONAL)

1 In nonstick 12-inch skillet, heat oil over medium-high heat until hot. Add onion, carrot, and garlic, and cook until vegetables are tender and golden, about 15 minutes, stirring occasionally. Add beans, broth, salt, pepper, and 2 teaspoons chopped sage; heat to boiling. Cover skillet and keep warm.

2 Meanwhile, cut each squash lengthwise in half and remove seeds and strings. Place squash halves in 3-quart microwave-safe baking dish. Cover and cook in microwave oven on High for 6 to 8 minutes, until squash is fork-tender.

3 Place squash halves, cut sides up, on platter. Fill each half with one-fourth of warm bean mixture; sprinkle with tomato and remaining 1 teaspoon chopped sage. Garnish with sage sprigs. Serve with Parmesan, if you like.

250 CALORIES

PER SERVING. 9G PROTEIN | 47G CARBOHYDRATE | 5G TOTAL FAT (1G SATURATED) 11G FIBER | 0MG CHOLESTEROL | 520MG SODIUM Ⓥ ⬙

MAKE IT A MEAL: These protein-packed "casseroles" make a cozy 455-calorie dinner when matched with Double Cornbread (125 calories; page 124) and a side of Green Beans with Mixed Mushrooms (80 calories; page 113).

MEXICAN VEGGIE STACKS

These Mexican-style stacks deliver a heaping helping of chili-spiced grilled vegetables, including fresh corn, tomatoes, onions, and zucchini.

ACTIVE TIME: 35 MINUTES · **TOTAL TIME:** 50 MINUTES
MAKES: 4 MAIN-DISH SERVINGS

2 TEASPOONS HOT MEXICAN-STYLE CHILI POWDER, OR 1 TABLESPOON REGULAR CHILI POWDER	1 METAL SKEWER
3 TABLESPOONS OLIVE OIL	1 LARGE RED ONION (12 OUNCES), CUT CROSSWISE INTO SLICES
¾ TEASPOON SALT	1 MEDIUM ZUCCHINI (8 OUNCES), CUT DIAGONALLY INTO ½-INCH-THICK SLICES
¼ CUP CHOPPED FRESH CILANTRO	
2 TABLESPOONS FRESH LIME JUICE	2 LARGE RIPE TOMATOES (10 TO 12 OUNCES EACH), EACH CUT HORIZONTALLY IN HALF
1 LARGE POBLANO CHILE (6 OUNCES)	
2 EARS CORN, HUSKS AND SILKS REMOVED	4 OUNCES MONTEREY JACK CHEESE, SHREDDED (1 CUP)

1 Prepare outdoor grill for direct grilling over medium-high heat.

2 In cup, combine chili powder, 2 tablespoons oil, and ½ teaspoon salt; set aside. In bowl, combine cilantro, lime juice, remaining ¼ teaspoon salt, and remaining 1 tablespoon oil; set aside.

3 Place poblano and corn on hot grill rack. Grill until poblano is blistered on all sides and corn is charred in spots, 10 to 15 minutes, turning occasionally.

4 Remove poblano from grill; wrap in foil, sealing tightly, and set aside to steam until cool enough to handle, about 15 minutes. Transfer corn to cutting board.

5 Push metal skewer horizontally through each onion slice to hold slice together. Brush both sides of onion and zucchini slices and cut sides of tomatoes with reserved chili oil; place on hot grill rack and cook until tender, about 10 minutes, turning over once. Place tomatoes on grill and cook until slightly softened, 6 to 8 minutes, turning over once. As vegetables are done, remove to platter and keep warm.

6 Unwrap poblano; remove stem and cut poblano lengthwise in half. Peel off skin and discard seeds, then cut into ¼-inch-wide strips. Cut corn from cobs; add to cilantro mixture.

7 Remove skewers from onion slices. On each plate, place 1 tomato half, cut side up. Place one-quarter of zucchini on top of each tomato; arrange half of cheese over zucchini. Arrange onion on top, separating into rings; sprinkle with remaining cheese, then poblano. Top with corn.

340 CALORIES **PER SERVING.** 13G PROTEIN | 31G CARBOHYDRATE | 21G TOTAL FAT (8G SATURATED) 6G FIBER | 30MG CHOLESTEROL | 670MG SODIUM

MAKE IT A MEAL: These stacks are so pretty and colorful. Pair them with our equally lovely Peach, Cucumber, and Barley Salad (145 calories; page 128) and you'll have a summery buffet for just 485 calories per serving.

RICOTTA-STUFFED PEPPERS

Jarred piquillo peppers—roasted, peeled, and ready to serve—are the time-saving secret behind this meatless main dish. Stuff with ricotta, then top with a simple basil pesto and toasted pine nuts.

ACTIVE TIME: 25 MINUTES · **TOTAL TIME:** 35 MINUTES
MAKES: 4 MAIN-DISH SERVINGS

1½ CUPS PART-SKIM RICOTTA CHEESE

¼ CUP FINELY GRATED PECORINO ROMANO CHEESE

1 GREEN ONION, GREEN PART ONLY, FINELY CHOPPED

3/8 TEASPOON SALT

3/8 TEASPOON GROUND BLACK PEPPER

12 WHOLE ROASTED RED PIQUILLO PEPPERS, PATTED DRY

½ CUP PACKED FRESH BASIL LEAVES

½ CUP PACKED FRESH FLAT-LEAF PARSLEY LEAVES

1 TABLESPOON WATER

3 TABLESPOONS EXTRA-VIRGIN OLIVE OIL

2 YELLOW SUMMER SQUASHES, THINLY SLICED INTO ROUNDS

2 TABLESPOONS PINE NUTS (PIGNOLI), TOASTED

1 In large bowl, using wire whisk, beat ricotta until smooth and fluffy. Gently stir in Pecorino, onion, and ¼ teaspoon each salt and pepper. Transfer filling to zip-tight plastic bag.

2 Snip off one corner of bag to make ½-inch hole. Into opening of 1 pepper, squeeze filling until pepper is full. Repeat with remaining peppers and filling. If making ahead, cover and refrigerate up to overnight.

3 In food processor, with knife blade attached, pulse basil, parsley, water, and remaining 1/8 teaspoon each salt and pepper until herbs are finely chopped. With machine running, add oil in steady stream; process until herb mixture forms smooth puree. If making ahead, cover and refrigerate up to overnight.

4 To serve, on large serving platter, arrange squash; place stuffed peppers on top. Stir sauce and spoon over peppers. Garnish with pine nuts.

320 CALORIES

PER SERVING. 15G PROTEIN | 17G CARBOHYDRATE | 22G TOTAL FAT (8G SATURATED) 3G FIBER | 36MG CHOLESTEROL | 615MG SODIUM

MAKE IT A MEAL: These stuffed peppers create an impressive platter. For an equally impressive finish, serve our individual Meyer Lemon Pudding Cakes (170 calories; page 146) for dessert. The complete meal costs just 490 calories.

COUSCOUS-STUFFED ARTICHOKES

Instead of topping your grains with veggies, why not *fill* your veggies with whole-grain goodness?

ACTIVE TIME: 1 HOUR · **TOTAL TIME:** 1 HOUR 15 MINUTES
MAKES: 4 MAIN-DISH SERVINGS

4   LARGE ARTICHOKES

1   TABLESPOON FRESH LEMON JUICE

3   TABLESPOONS OLIVE OIL

2   MEDIUM CARROTS, PEELED AND DICED

2   GARLIC CLOVES, MINCED

¼   CUP CHOPPED FRESH MINT

3   TABLESPOONS CHOPPED FRESH PARSLEY

1   CUP WHOLE-WHEAT COUSCOUS (MOROCCAN PASTA)

1½ CUPS CANNED OR HOMEMADE VEGETABLE BROTH (PAGE 37)

½   TEASPOON SALT

¼   TEASPOON COARSELY GROUND BLACK PEPPER

1   LEMON, CUT INTO WEDGES

PARSLEY SPRIGS FOR GARNISH

1 With sharp knife, cut 1 inch straight across tops of artichokes. Cut off stems so artichokes can stand upright. Reserve and peel stems. Pull off outer dark green leaves from artichoke bottoms. Using kitchen shears, trim thorny leaf tips.

2 Spread artichokes open and carefully cut around chokes with small knife; scrape out center petals and fuzzy center portions with teaspoon and discard. Rinse artichokes well.

3 In 5-quart saucepot, heat lemon juice and 1 *inch water* to boiling over high heat. Set artichokes on stem ends in boiling water, along with peeled stems; return to boiling. Reduce heat to low; cover and simmer until knife inserted in center goes through bottom easily, 30 to 40 minutes. Drain.

4 Meanwhile, preheat oven to 400°F.

5 In nonstick 10-inch skillet, heat 1 tablespoon oil over medium heat until hot. Add carrots and cook until tender, about 10 minutes, stirring occasionally. Stir in garlic; cook 1 minute longer. Remove to medium bowl. When artichoke stems are cooked through, dice and add to carrot mixture with mint and parsley.

6 Prepare couscous as label directs but use 1 cup broth in place of equal amount water. When couscous is done, stir in salt, pepper, carrot mixture, and remaining 2 tablespoons oil.

7 Pour remaining ½ cup broth into shallow baking dish large enough to hold all artichokes (13" by 9"); arrange cooked artichokes in dish. Spoon couscous mixture between artichoke leaves and into center cavities. Bake until artichokes are heated through, 15 to 20 minutes.

8 Serve artichokes with lemon wedges and garnish with parsley sprigs.

350 CALORIES **PER SERVING.** 11G PROTEIN | 54G CARBOHYDRATE | 11G TOTAL FAT (2G SATURATED) 12G FIBER | 4MG CHOLESTEROL | 600MG SODIUM ⓥ 🌾

MAKE IT A MEAL: For a Mediterranean-style dinner, nibble on three or four Kalamata olives (30 calories) as a starter, then serve these grain-stuffed artichokes with a hearty side of Roasted Cauliflower (70 calories; page 110) or Root Vegetable Gratin (145 calories; page 117).

STUFFED PORTOBELLOS

This healthy meal is low in calories, yet hearty enough to serve as a main course. Meaty portobello mushrooms combine with protein-rich quinoa, creamy feta, and vitamin-dense Brussels sprouts to create a flavorful dish packed with nutrients. Quinoa, which has a mild, slightly nutty flavor, packs more protein than any other grain.

TOTAL TIME: 30 MINUTES
MAKES: 4 MAIN-DISH SERVINGS

½ CUP QUINOA, RINSED	1 TEASPOON FRESH THYME LEAVES, FINELY CHOPPED
¾ CUP WATER	⅔ CUP FROZEN CORN
1¼ POUNDS BRUSSELS SPROUTS	3 OUNCES FETA CHEESE, CRUMBLED (¾ CUP)
4 TEASPOONS EXTRA-VIRGIN OLIVE OIL	½ TEASPOON GROUND CUMIN
⅜ TEASPOON SALT	
¼ TEASPOON GROUND BLACK PEPPER	
4 LARGE PORTOBELLO MUSHROOM CAPS (1 POUND)	

1 Preheat oven to 450°F. In 2-quart saucepan, combine quinoa and water. Heat to boiling over high heat; reduce heat to medium-low. Cover and cook 15 minutes or until liquid is absorbed.

2 Meanwhile, trim and halve sprouts. In 18" by 12" jelly-roll pan, toss sprouts, 2 teaspoons oil, and ¼ teaspoon each salt and pepper. Roast 10 minutes.

3 Meanwhile, brush mushrooms with remaining 2 teaspoons oil and sprinkle with remaining ⅛ teaspoon salt. Combine thyme, corn, feta, cumin, and cooked quinoa in medium bowl.

4 When sprouts have roasted 10 minutes, push to one side of pan and arrange mushrooms, gill sides up, on other side. Divide quinoa mixture among mushrooms; roast 10 minutes or until mushrooms are tender.

290 CALORIES

PER SERVING. 14G PROTEIN | 38G CARBOHYDRATE | 11G TOTAL FAT (4G SATURATED) 9G FIBER | 19MG CHOLESTEROL | 500MG SODIUM ☻ ⦿

MAKE IT A MEAL: You can't go wrong with this protein- and vitamin-packed plate. For a fresh, pretty first course, add on our Mesclun with Pears and Pumpkin Seeds (100 calories; page 114) to create a 390-calorie meal.

FAST FRIED RICE

Who needs Chinese takeout when you can make a low-cal veggie fried rice at home with such ease? The secrets to this easy weeknight dish are quick-cooking brown rice, precut frozen vegetables, and ready-to-use stir-fry sauce.

TOTAL TIME: 20 MINUTES

MAKES: 4 MAIN-DISH SERVINGS

1½ CUPS INSTANT (10-MINUTE) BROWN RICE

1 PACKAGE (16 OUNCES) FIRM TOFU, DRAINED AND CUT INTO 1-INCH CUBES

6 TEASPOONS OLIVE OIL

1 PACKAGE (16 OUNCES) FROZEN VEGETABLES FOR STIR-FRY

2 LARGE EGGS, LIGHTLY BEATEN

½ CUP STIR-FRY SAUCE

¼ CUP WATER

1 In medium saucepan, prepare rice as label directs.

2 Meanwhile, place three layers of paper towels in medium bowl. Place tofu on towels and top with three more layers paper towels. Gently press tofu with hands to extract excess moisture.

3 In 12-inch skillet, heat 2 teaspoons oil over medium-high heat until hot. Add frozen vegetables; cover and cook 5 minutes, stirring occasionally. Transfer vegetables to bowl; keep warm.

4 In same skillet, heat remaining 4 teaspoons oil until hot. Add tofu and cook 5 minutes, gently stirring. Stir in rice and cook 4 minutes longer.

5 With spatula, push rice mixture around edge of skillet, leaving space in center. Add eggs to center of skillet; cook 1 minute, stirring eggs until scrambled. Add stir-fry sauce, vegetables, and water; cook 1 minute, stirring. Serve immediately.

360 CALORIES

PER SERVING. 17G PROTEIN | 41G CARBOHYDRATE | 15G TOTAL FAT (2G SATURATED) 5G FIBER | 106MG CHOLESTEROL | 760MG SODIUM 💚 🌱

MAKE IT A MEAL: Add a side of our Crunchy Peanut Broccoli (150 calories; page 119) to create a yummy 510-calorie dinner.

SWEET-AND-SOUR UNSTUFFED CABBAGE

These cabbage wedges are microwaved, then topped with a sweet-and-sour tomato sauce—a simplified version of classic stuffed cabbage.

ACTIVE TIME: 20 MINUTES · **TOTAL TIME:** 40 MINUTES
MAKES: 4 MAIN-DISH SERVINGS

1 SMALL HEAD SAVOY CABBAGE (1½ POUNDS)	3 GREEN ONIONS, THINLY SLICED
¼ CUP WATER	1 TABLESPOON MINCED, PEELED FRESH GINGER
1 TABLESPOON OLIVE OIL	1 CAN (14½ OUNCES) DICED TOMATOES
2 MEDIUM CARROTS, PEELED AND CHOPPED	2 TABLESPOONS SOY SAUCE
2 STALKS CELERY, CHOPPED	2 TABLESPOONS SEASONED RICE VINEGAR
1 MEDIUM RED PEPPER (4 TO 6 OUNCES), CHOPPED	1 TABLESPOON PACKED LIGHT BROWN SUGAR
3 GARLIC CLOVES, CRUSHED WITH GARLIC PRESS	

1 Discard tough outer leaves from cabbage; core and cut cabbage into 4 wedges. Place wedges and water in 3-quart microwave-safe dish; cover and cook in microwave oven on High for 12 to 14 minutes, until fork-tender.
2 Meanwhile, in nonstick 12-inch skillet, heat oil over medium-high heat until hot. Add carrots, celery, and red pepper; cook until vegetables are tender and golden, about 12 minutes. Add garlic, green onions, and ginger; cook 2 minutes, stirring. Add tomatoes with their juice, soy sauce, vinegar, and brown sugar; heat to boiling over medium-high heat. Reduce heat to medium-low and simmer 5 minutes, stirring occasionally.
3 Spoon tomato mixture over cabbage in baking dish; cover and cook in microwave on High for 2 minutes to blend flavors.

145 CALORIES

PER SERVING. 6G PROTEIN | 26G CARBOHYDRATE | 4G TOTAL FAT (1G SATURATED)
7G FIBER | 0MG CHOLESTEROL | 1,200MG SODIUM ✔ ❀

> **MAKE IT A MEAL:** Brown rice seasoned with lemon juice and parsley (215 calories per serving) makes the perfect base for this sweet-and-sour cabbage. Finish with one of our oatmeal-raisin cookies (65 calories; page 159) for a comforting meal that's just 425 calories per serving.

LO MEIN WITH TOFU, SNOW PEAS, AND CARROTS

Packaged ramen noodles can be a great short-cut ingredient. Here they're combined with tofu, snow peas, carrots, and bean sprouts for a tasty homemade lo mein.

TOTAL TIME: 15 MINUTES PLUS DRAINING TOFU

MAKES: 4 MAIN-DISH SERVINGS

2 PACKAGES (3 OUNCES EACH) ORIENTAL-FLAVOR RAMEN NOODLES

2 TEASPOONS VEGETABLE OIL

1 PACKAGE (16 OUNCES) EXTRA-FIRM TOFU, DRAINED AND PRESSED (SEE PAGE 15), DICED

6 OUNCES (2 CUPS) SNOW PEAS, STRINGS REMOVED AND EACH CUT DIAGONALLY IN HALF

3 GREEN ONIONS, CUT INTO 2-INCH PIECES

1 PACKAGE (5 OUNCES) SHREDDED CARROTS (1½ CUPS)

½ CUP BOTTLED STIR-FRY SAUCE

3 OUNCES FRESH BEAN SPROUTS (1 CUP), RINSED AND DRAINED

1 Heat 4-quart covered saucepot of *water* to boiling over high heat. Add ramen noodles (reserve flavor packets) and cook 2 minutes. Drain noodles, reserving *¼ cup cooking water*.

2 Meanwhile, in nonstick 12-inch skillet, heat oil over medium heat until hot. Add tofu and cook until lightly browned, 6 to 8 minutes, gently stirring a few times. Add snow peas and green onions; cook until vegetables are tender-crisp, 3 to 5 minutes, stirring frequently. Stir in carrots, stir-fry sauce, and contents of 1 ramen flavor packet to taste (depending on salt level of sauce); cook until carrots are tender, 2 to 3 minutes. (Discard remaining flavor packet or save for another use.)

3 Reserve some bean sprouts for garnish. Add noodles, reserved noodle cooking water, and remaining bean sprouts to skillet; cook 1 minute to blend flavors, stirring. Sprinkle with reserved bean sprouts to serve.

375 CALORIES

PER SERVING. 18G PROTEIN | 47G CARBOHYDRATE | 12G TOTAL FAT (3G SATURATED) 4G FIBER | 0MG CHOLESTEROL | 1,485MG SODIUM Ⓥ

MAKE IT A MEAL: For a super-fast takeout-style meal that comes in under 500 calories, nibble on some steamed edamame (100 calories for 1 cup) before digging into the yummy noodle dish.

310 CALORIES

Vegetable Lasagna
(page 76)

PASTAS, GRAINS & CASSEROLES

If you associate pasta and casseroles with a growing bulge around your middle, try these low-calorie recipes on for size. Pasta dishes like Farfalle with Baby Artichokes and Mushrooms and Spaghetti with Beets and Greens are bursting with vitamin-packed seasonal vegetables; you can swap in wholesome whole-wheat noodles, if you like. Even our trio of lasagnas contain loads of vegetables, plus cheese for added richness. If you've only enjoyed risotto in a restaurant, try our super-easy Summer Tomato Risotto: This pretty, company-worthy dish is prepared in the microwave for maximum ease.

KEY TO ICONS

30 minutes or less V Vegan ♥ Heart healthy High fiber Make ahead

FARFALLE WITH BABY ARTICHOKES AND MUSHROOMS

These baby artichokes harness the sweet, rich flavor of their full-grown counterparts, without requiring you to remove the inedible center thistle, or "choke." When cut, uncooked artichokes discolor quickly—be sure to rub lemon on any exposed surfaces.

ACTIVE TIME: 30 MINUTES · **TOTAL TIME:** 1 HOUR
MAKES: 6 MAIN-DISH SERVINGS

1 POUND FARFALLE OR ORECHIETTE PASTA	1 CUP CANNED OR HOMEMADE VEGETABLE BROTH (PAGE 37)
1 LEMON, CUT IN HALF	½ CUP DRY WHITE WINE
1 POUND (ABOUT 14) BABY ARTICHOKES	1 TABLESPOON CHOPPED FRESH THYME LEAVES
2 TABLESPOONS OLIVE OIL	
1 PACKAGE (10 OUNCES) SLICED MUSHROOMS	2 TABLESPOONS CHOPPED FRESH PARSLEY LEAVES
½ TEASPOON SALT	FRESHLY GRATED PARMESAN CHEESE (OPTIONAL)
¼ TEASPOON GROUND BLACK PEPPER	
2 GARLIC CLOVES, CRUSHED WITH GARLIC PRESS	

1 Cook pasta as label directs and reserve ¼ *cup cooking water* before draining.

2 Meanwhile, in covered nonstick 12-inch skillet, heat 1 *inch water* to boiling over high heat. Fill medium bowl with cold water and add juice of 1 lemon half.

3 Trim artichokes: Bend back outer green leaves and snap off at base until remaining leaves are green on top and yellow on bottom. Cut off top half of each artichoke and discard. Rub cut surfaces with remaining lemon half to prevent browning. With vegetable peeler, peel stems. Cut off stems level with bottom of artichoke and coarsely chop stems; add to bowl of lemon water. Cut each artichoke into quarters; add to lemon water.

4 Drain artichokes and stems and place in boiling water in skillet. Cook, covered, 8 to 10 minutes or until artichokes are tender when pierced with tip of small knife. Drain well and set aside.

5 Dry skillet with paper towel. Add oil to skillet and heat over medium-high heat until hot. Add mushrooms, salt, and pepper, and cook about 3 minutes or until mushrooms begin to soften, stirring occasionally. Add artichoke pieces and garlic, and cook about 5 minutes longer or until mushrooms are lightly browned and artichokes are very tender. Stir broth, wine, and thyme into skillet, and heat to boiling; boil 1 minute. Stir in parsley.
6 When pasta is done, add to skillet with artichokes and mushrooms. Cook 1 minute to blend flavors, tossing to combine. Stir in reserved cooking water if pasta is dry. Serve with grated Parmesan, if you like.

360 CALORIES | **PER SERVING.** 13G PROTEIN | 63G CARBOHYDRATE | 6G TOTAL FAT (1G SATURATED) 4G FIBER | 0MG CHOLESTEROL | 495MG SODIUM Ⓥ

MAKE IT A MEAL: For a colorful finish to a 485-calorie Italian dinner, serve Berries in Red Wine (125 calories; page 141) for dessert.

MIDDLE-EASTERN GARBANZO BEANS AND MACARONI

Here's a flavorful entrée based on pantry staples—canned chickpeas and crushed tomatoes—tossed with pasta.

ACTIVE TIME: 10 MINUTES · **TOTAL TIME:** 35 MINUTES
MAKES: 6 MAIN-DISH SERVINGS

12 OUNCES MACARONI TWISTS OR ELBOW MACARONI

1 TABLESPOON OLIVE OIL

1 TABLESPOON BUTTER OR MARGARINE

1 LARGE ONION (12 OUNCES), CUT INTO ¼-INCH PIECES

2 GARLIC CLOVES, CRUSHED WITH GARLIC PRESS

1 TEASPOON SALT

1 TEASPOON GROUND CUMIN

¾ TEASPOON GROUND CORIANDER

¼ TEASPOON GROUND ALLSPICE

¼ TEASPOON COARSELY GROUND BLACK PEPPER

1 CAN (28 OUNCES) CRUSHED TOMATOES

1 CAN (15 TO 19 OUNCES) GARBANZO BEANS, RINSED AND DRAINED

¼ CUP LOOSELY PACKED FRESH PARSLEY LEAVES, CHOPPED

PARSLEY SPRIGS FOR GARNISH

1 In large saucepot, cook pasta as label directs.

2 Meanwhile, in nonstick 12-inch skillet, heat oil with butter over medium heat until hot and melted. Add onion and cook, stirring occasionally, until tender and golden, about 20 minutes. Stir in garlic, salt, cumin, coriander, allspice, and pepper; cook 1 minute.

3 Add tomatoes and garbanzos to skillet; heat to boiling over medium-high heat. Reduce heat to medium-low; simmer, stirring occasionally, 5 minutes.

4 Drain pasta; return to saucepot. Toss garbanzo-bean mixture with pasta; heat through. Toss with chopped parsley just before serving. Garnish with parsley sprigs.

400 CALORIES

PER SERVING. 14G PROTEIN | 73G CARBOHYDRATE | 7G TOTAL FAT (2G SATURATED) 5G FIBER | 5MG CHOLESTEROL | 1,039MG SODIUM

MAKE IT A MEAL: Add on a side of Sautéed Spinach with Garlic and Lemon (45 calories; page 109) to round out this hearty 445-calorie dinner.

PASTA WITH SPINACH-CHIVE PESTO

We're all familiar with the classic pesto made from fresh basil leaves, olive-oil, pine nuts, and Parmesan cheese. But did you know you can make pesto sauce from other fresh herbs and even tender greens like baby spinach? This garden-fresh recipe teaches you how.

ACTIVE TIME: 10 MINUTES · **TOTAL TIME:** 40 MINUTES

MAKES: 4 MAIN-DISH SERVINGS

1 PACKAGE (16 OUNCES) RIGATONI OR PENNE

2 CUPS BABY SPINACH LEAVES

1½ CUPS FRESH FLAT-LEAF PARSLEY LEAVES

¼ CUP CHOPPED FRESH CHIVES

3 TABLESPOONS EXTRA-VIRGIN OLIVE OIL

¼ CUP PINE NUTS (PIGNOLI), PLUS ADDITIONAL FOR GARNISH

¼ TEASPOON SALT

¼ CUP FRESHLY GRATED PARMESAN CHEESE, PLUS FRESHLY SHAVED PARMESAN FOR GARNISH

1 Cook pasta as label directs, then drain and return to cooking pot.

2 Meanwhile, in blender, combine spinach, parsley, chives, oil, pine nuts, and salt. Puree pesto until smooth. Stir in grated Parmesan (see Tip).

3 Transfer pasta to large serving bowl. Add pesto to pasta; toss to combine. Top with shaved Parmesan and additional pine nuts.

TIP If you aren't serving the pesto immediately, don't add the grated Parmesan. Refrigerate the pesto in an airtight container for up to two days or freeze it for up to two months and stir in the cheese before serving.

395 CALORIES

PER SERVING. 12G PROTEIN | 48G CARBOHYDRATE | 18G TOTAL FAT (3G SATURATED) 4G FIBER | 4MG CHOLESTEROL | 282MG SODIUM ♥ ▤

MAKE IT A MEAL: For a light summer supper, pair this delicate pasta with a wedge of cantaloupe dressed with a squeeze of lime (25 calories). Enjoy the whole meal for just 420 calories.

SPAGHETTI WITH BEETS AND GREENS

In this innovative dish, garlicky beets and their greens are tossed with spaghetti, tinting the pasta a beautiful pinkish-red! If you're not going to use beets immediately, trim the tops ahead of time, since the leaves leach moisture and color from the beets. Refrigerate the greens and the beets in separate plastic bags and use them within two days.

ACTIVE TIME: 20 MINUTES · **TOTAL TIME:** 35 MINUTES

MAKES: 6 MAIN-DISH SERVINGS

2	BUNCHES BEETS WITH TOPS (ABOUT 3 POUNDS TOTAL)	2	GARLIC CLOVES, CRUSHED WITH GARLIC PRESS
½	CUP WATER	⅛	TEASPOON CRUSHED RED PEPPER
1	PACKAGE (16 OUNCES) SPAGHETTI	1	TEASPOON SALT
3	TABLESPOONS OLIVE OIL		

1 Cut tops from beets and set greens aside. If beets are not uniform in size, cut larger beets in half. Place beets and water in deep 3-quart microwave-safe baking dish; cover and cook in microwave oven on High for 15 to 20 minutes, or until beets are tender when pierced with tip of knife. Rinse beets under cold running water until cool enough to handle. Peel beets; cut into ½-inch pieces.

2 Meanwhile, in large saucepot, cook spaghetti as label directs. Trim and discard stems from beet greens. Coarsely chop beet greens; set aside.

3 In nonstick 12-inch skillet, heat oil, garlic, and crushed red pepper over medium heat 5 minutes or until garlic is lightly golden. Increase heat to medium-high; add beet greens and cook 3 minutes, stirring. Add beets and salt and cook 1 to 2 minutes or until mixture is hot.

4 When spaghetti is done, reserve ¾ cup pasta cooking water, then drain and return pasta to pot. Add beet mixture and reserved water; toss.

375 **PER SERVING.** 11G PROTEIN | 64G CARBOHYDRATE | 8G TOTAL FAT (1G SATURATED)
CALORIES 5G FIBER | 0MG CHOLESTEROL | 570MG SODIUM ⓥ ✿

MAKE IT A MEAL: To keep the red theme, finish the meal with Berries in Red Wine (125 calories; page 141) for a jewel-like 500-calorie dinner.

VEGETABLE LASAGNA

This lasagna is loaded with veggies. For photo, see page 68.

ACTIVE TIME: 25 MINUTES · **TOTAL TIME:** 1 HOUR 15 MINUTES

MAKES: 4 MAIN-DISH SERVINGS

2   MEDIUM ZUCCHINI OR YELLOW SUMMER SQUASHES (8 OUNCES EACH), THINLY SLICED

1   TABLESPOON OLIVE OIL

¼   TEASPOON SALT

1   BUNCH SWISS CHARD, TOUGH STEMS DISCARDED, THINLY SLICED

1   SMALL ONION, FINELY CHOPPED

2   GARLIC CLOVES, CRUSHED WITH GARLIC PRESS

1   TEASPOON FRESH THYME LEAVES, CHOPPED

1   POUND PLUM TOMATOES, CORED AND THINLY SLICED

4   NO-BOIL LASAGNA NOODLES, RINSED WITH COLD WATER

2   CARROTS, PEELED AND SHREDDED

1   CUP PART-SKIM RICOTTA CHEESE

2   OUNCES PROVOLONE CHEESE, FINELY SHREDDED (½ CUP)

1   Arrange one oven rack 4 inches from broiler heat source and place second rack in center. Preheat broiler.

2   In large bowl, toss zucchini with 1 teaspoon oil and ⅛ teaspoon salt. Arrange on 18" by 12" jelly-roll pan in single layer. Broil 6 minutes or until golden brown, turning over once. Set aside. Reset oven control to 425°F.

3   Rinse chard in cold water; drain, leaving some water clinging to leaves.

4   In 12-inch skillet, heat remaining 2 teaspoons oil over medium heat. Add onion; cook 3 minutes or until soft, stirring occasionally. Add chard, garlic, thyme, and remaining ⅛ teaspoon salt. Cook 6 to 7 minutes or until chard is very soft, stirring frequently. Remove from heat and set aside.

5   In 8-inch square baking dish, layer half of tomatoes, lasagna noodles, Swiss chard, shredded carrots, zucchini slices, and ricotta, in that order. Repeat layering once. Top with provolone. Cover with foil. (Lasagna can be prepared to this point and refrigerated up to overnight.) Bake 30 minutes, covered (if refrigerated, bake 10 minutes longer). Uncover and bake 20 minutes longer or until golden brown and bubbling.

310 CALORIES   **PER SERVING.** 17G PROTEIN | 33G CARBOHYDRATE | 13G TOTAL FAT (6G SATURATED) 6G FIBER | 29MG CHOLESTEROL | 520MG SODIUM

MAKE IT A MEAL: Artichokes with Creamy Lemon Sauce (145 calories; page 118) are just the thing to complete a 455-calorie lasagna dinner.

POLENTA LASAGNA

This stress-free casserole is perfect for a last-minute dinner party.

ACTIVE TIME: 45 MINUTES · **TOTAL TIME:** 1 HOUR 15 MINUTES PLUS STANDING
MAKES: 6 MAIN-DISH SERVINGS

1   TABLESPOON OLIVE OIL

1   SMALL ONION, FINELY CHOPPED

1   GARLIC CLOVE, MINCED

1   CAN (28 OUNCES) TOMATOES

2   TABLESPOONS TOMATO PASTE

2   TABLESPOONS CHOPPED FRESH BASIL

1   TEASPOON SALT

1   PACKAGE (10 OUNCES) FROZEN CHOPPED SPINACH, THAWED AND SQUEEZED DRY

1   CUP PART-SKIM RICOTTA CHEESE

2   TABLESPOONS FRESHLY GRATED PARMESAN CHEESE

¼   TEASPOON COARSELY GROUND BLACK PEPPER

1   LOG (24 OUNCES) PRECOOKED PLAIN POLENTA, CUT INTO 16 SLICES

4   OUNCES PART-SKIM MOZZARELLA CHEESE, SHREDDED (1 CUP)

1   In 3-quart saucepan, heat oil over medium heat. Add onion and cook until tender, about 8 minutes, stirring occasionally. Add garlic and cook 30 seconds longer. Stir in tomatoes with their juice, tomato paste, basil, and ½ teaspoon salt; heat to boiling over high heat. Reduce heat to low and simmer, uncovered, 20 minutes, stirring occasionally and breaking up tomatoes with side of spoon. Set sauce aside.

2   Meanwhile, in medium bowl, mix spinach, ricotta, Parmesan, pepper, and remaining ½ teaspoon salt until blended.

3   Preheat oven to 350°F. Grease 8-inch square glass baking dish.

4   Arrange half of polenta slices, overlapping, in baking dish. Drop half of spinach mixture, by rounded tablespoons, on top of polenta (mixture will not completely cover slices). Spread half of sauce on top to form an even layer. Sprinkle with half of mozzarella. Repeat layering.

5   Bake casserole until hot and bubbling, about 30 minutes. Let stand 10 minutes for easier serving.

270
CALORIES

PER SERVING. 16G PROTEIN | 3G CARBOHYDRATE | 10G TOTAL FAT (15G SATURATED) 4G FIBER | 28MG CHOLESTEROL | 1,210MG SODIUM

MAKE IT A MEAL: For a perfect autumn meal, serve with our Mesclun with Pears and Pumpkin Seeds (100 calories; page 114). You can enjoy it all for just 370 calories!

BUTTERNUT SQUASH AND SAGE LASAGNA

With our freeze-now, serve-later dishes, you can serve a comfy meal on even the busiest weeknight. The light, minty flavor of fresh sage pairs beautifully with sweet butternut squash in this special entrée.

ACTIVE TIME: 50 MINUTES · **TOTAL TIME:** 2 HOURS

MAKES: 2 CASSEROLES OR 12 MAIN-DISH SERVINGS

---

2 LARGE ONIONS (12 OUNCES EACH), EACH CUT IN HALF, THEN CUT CROSSWISE INTO ¼-INCH SLICES

2 TABLESPOONS OLIVE OIL

1½ TEASPOONS SALT

¾ TEASPOON COARSELY GROUND BLACK PEPPER

2 MEDIUM BUTTERNUT SQUASHES (1¾ POUNDS EACH), EACH CUT IN HALF AND SEEDED

7 CUPS LOW-FAT MILK (1%)

½ CUP CORNSTARCH

¼ CUP PACKED FRESH SAGE LEAVES, CHOPPED

¼ TEASPOON GROUND NUTMEG

2 CUPS FRESHLY GRATED PARMESAN CHEESE

12 NO-BOIL LASAGNA NOODLES

3 PACKAGES (10 OUNCES EACH) FROZEN CHOPPED SPINACH, THAWED AND SQUEEZED DRY

1 Preheat oven to 450°F. In large bowl, toss onions with oil, ¼ teaspoon salt, and ¼ teaspoon pepper. Place onions in one 15½" by 10½" jelly-roll pan. Line a second jelly-roll pan with foil; arrange squash in pan, cut sides up. Sprinkle with ¼ teaspoon salt and ¼ teaspoon pepper. Cover squash pan tightly with aluminum foil. (Do not cover onions.) Roast both pans 45 minutes or until squash is tender and onions are browned, stirring onions halfway through cooking. Reset oven control to 375°F.

2 Meanwhile, in 5-quart saucepot (do not use smaller pot; milk mixture may boil over), heat 6 cups milk over medium-high heat just to simmering, stirring occasionally. In small bowl, whisk cornstarch into remaining 1 cup milk. Add cornstarch mixture to simmering milk; heat to full rolling boil and cook 1 minute, stirring constantly and scraping bottom of pot to prevent scorching. Remove from heat; stir in sage, nutmeg, 1½ cups Parmesan, and remaining 1 teaspoon salt and ¼ teaspoon pepper.

3 When vegetables are done, scrape squash flesh out of skins and into food processor with knife blade attached; discard skins. Add onions; puree until smooth. Makes about 4 cups puree.

4 Into each of two 8-inch square glass or ceramic baking dishes, spoon ½ cup white sauce to cover bottoms. Arrange 2 lasagna noodles over sauce in each casserole. Evenly spread 1 cup squash puree, then ¾ cup chopped spinach over noodles in each casserole. Top each with 1 cup sauce. Repeat layering one time, starting with noodles. Top each with 2 more noodles. Spread remaining sauce on top; sprinkle with remaining Parmesan.

5 Cover one casserole with aluminum foil. Place on cookie sheet (to catch any spills) and bake 30 minutes. Uncover and bake 15 minutes longer or until hot and bubbly. Let stand 10 minutes for easier serving. Wrap second casserole in plastic and freeze until solid; then remove from dish, wrap tightly with heavy-duty foil, label, and freeze for up to 3 months.

335 **PER SERVING.** 17G PROTEIN | 46G CARBOHYDRATE | 10G TOTAL FAT (4G SATURATED)
CALORIES 5G FIBER | 17MG CHOLESTEROL | 730MG SODIUM ♥ 🍴

MAKE IT A MEAL: Make the lasagna ahead of time and reheat when you're ready to serve. Our Greens with Goat Cheese and Tangerine Vinaigrette (165 calories; page 121) is all you need to round out a quick 500-calorie dinner.

BULGUR PILAF WITH APRICOTS

A hint of curry transforms this simple grain and bean pilaf.

ACTIVE TIME: 10 MINUTES · **TOTAL TIME:** 30 MINUTES
MAKES: 4 MAIN-DISH SERVINGS

¾ CUP WATER

1 CAN (14½ OUNCES) VEGETABLE BROTH OR 1¾ CUPS HOMEMADE BROTH (PAGE 37)

1 CUP BULGUR

1 TABLESPOON OLIVE OIL

1 SMALL ONION, CHOPPED

2 TEASPOONS CURRY POWDER

1 GARLIC CLOVE, CRUSHED WITH GARLIC PRESS

1 CAN (15 TO 19 OUNCES) GARBANZO BEANS (CHICKPEAS), RINSED AND DRAINED

½ CUP DRIED APRICOTS, CHOPPED

½ TEASPOON SALT

¼ CUP LOOSELY PACKED FRESH PARSLEY LEAVES, CHOPPED

1 In 2-quart covered saucepan, heat water and 1¼ cups vegetable broth to boiling on high. Stir in bulgur; heat to boiling. Reduce heat to medium-low; cover and simmer 12 to 15 minutes or until liquid is absorbed. Remove saucepan from heat. Uncover and fluff with fork to separate grains.

2 Meanwhile, in nonstick 12-inch skillet, heat oil over medium heat. Add onion and cook 10 minutes, stirring occasionally. Stir in curry powder and garlic; cook 1 minute.

3 Stir in garbanzo beans, apricots, salt, and remaining ½ cup vegetable broth; heat to boiling. Remove saucepan from heat; stir in bulgur and parsley.

370 CALORIES

PER SERVING. 13G PROTEIN | 71G CARBOHYDRATE | 6G TOTAL FAT (1G SATURATED) 15G FIBER | 0MG CHOLESTEROL | 815MG SODIUM ♥ Ⓥ ⚘ ▬

MAKE IT A MEAL: For a sweet and fruity finish to this tasty pilaf, try our Three-Fruit Salad with Vanilla Syrup (140 calories; page 143).

VEGETABLE COBBLER

What a satisfying, savory twist on fruit cobbler! Here winter vegetables are roasted until tender, then bathed in a lightened cream sauce (no cream here, though—it's made with low-fat milk) and topped with biscuit dough baked to golden-brown goodness.

ACTIVE TIME: 15 MINUTES · **TOTAL TIME:** 1 HOUR 30 MINUTES

MAKES: 6 MAIN-DISH SERVINGS

1   MEDIUM BUTTERNUT SQUASH (1¾ POUNDS), PEELED, SEEDED, AND CUT INTO 1½-INCH CHUNKS

1   POUND RED POTATOES (3 LARGE), CUT INTO 1½-INCH CHUNKS (SEE TIP)

3   MEDIUM PARSNIPS, PEELED AND CUT INTO 1-INCH PIECES

1   MEDIUM RED ONION, CUT INTO 6 WEDGES

¾   TEASPOON SALT

½   TEASPOON DRIED TARRAGON

2   TABLESPOONS OLIVE OIL

1   CAN (14½ OUNCES) VEGETABLE BROTH OR 1¾ CUPS HOMEMADE BROTH (PAGE 37)

½   TEASPOON FRESHLY GRATED LEMON PEEL

1   SMALL BUNCH (12 OUNCES) BROCCOLI, CUT INTO 2" BY 1" PIECES

½   CUP PLUS ⅔ CUP LOW-FAT MILK (1%)

1   TABLESPOON CORNSTARCH

1¾ CUPS ALL-PURPOSE BAKING MIX

½   CUP CORNMEAL

¾   TEASPOON COARSELY GROUND BLACK PEPPER

1   Preheat oven to 450°F. In shallow 3½- to 4-quart casserole or 13" by 9" glass baking dish, toss squash, potatoes, parsnips, onion, salt, and tarragon with oil until well coated. Bake until vegetables are fork-tender and lightly browned, about 1 hour, stirring once.

2   After vegetables have cooked 45 minutes, in 3-quart saucepan, heat broth and lemon peel to boiling over high heat. Add broccoli; return to boiling. Reduce heat to low; cover and simmer broccoli 1 minute.

3   In cup, with fork or wire whisk, stir ½ cup milk with cornstarch until blended. Combine milk and broccoli mixtures, stirring constantly, until liquid boils and thickens slightly; boil 1 minute. Pour broccoli mixture over vegetables; stir until brown bits are loosened from bottom of casserole.

4 In medium bowl, stir together baking mix, cornmeal, pepper, and remaining ⅔ cup milk until just combined. Drop 12 heaping spoonfuls biscuit dough on top of vegetable mixture. Continue baking cobbler until biscuits are browned, about 15 minutes.

TIP You can peel the potatoes, but leaving the skin on during cooking is the best way to conserve their nutrients. If you do peel them, keep the peelings as thin as possible.

395 CALORIES

PER SERVING. 11G PROTEIN | 67G CARBOHYDRATE | 11G TOTAL FAT (2G SATURATED) 8G FIBER | 5MG CHOLESTEROL | 940MG SODIUM 🌐 🍲

MAKE IT A MEAL: Serve with a crunchy salad of Romaine hearts, sliced, three Bosc pears, sliced, tossed with 3 tablespoons each olive oil and lemon juice, and ¼ teaspoon each salt and pepper. Top with 2 tablespoons toasted walnuts. The salad is 130 calories per serving; enjoy it with the cobbler for a 525-calorie meal.

SUMMER TOMATO RISOTTO

Heat-beating and hands-off, this risotto, featuring the summer bounty of corn and tomatoes, is simmered in the microwave from beginning to end, so there's no endless toiling over a steamy stove.

ACTIVE TIME: 30 MINUTES · **TOTAL TIME:** 40 MINUTES
MAKES: 6 MAIN-DISH SERVINGS

1   BAG (12 OUNCES) MICROWAVE-IN-BAG GREEN BEANS

1   CAN (14½ OUNCES) REDUCED-SODIUM VEGETABLE BROTH OR 1¾ CUPS HOMEMADE BROTH (PAGE 37)

2   CUPS WATER

2   TABLESPOONS BUTTER

1   SMALL ONION, CHOPPED

2   CUPS ARBORIO RICE

2   POUNDS RIPE TOMATOES

2   CUPS FRESH CORN KERNELS

2   OUNCES FINELY GRATED PARMESAN CHEESE

½   TEASPOON SALT

¼   TEASPOON GROUND BLACK PEPPER

2   TABLESPOONS CHOPPED BASIL

1   Cook beans as label directs. Cool slightly; cut into 1 inch pieces.

2   In 2-quart saucepan, heat broth and water to boiling.

3   Meanwhile, in 4-quart microwave-safe bowl, microwave butter and onion, uncovered, on High for 3 minutes. Stir in rice. Cook on High for 1 minute. Stir in broth. Cover with vented plastic wrap; microwave on Medium (50% power) 10 minutes.

4   Meanwhile, in food processor, puree half of tomatoes; strain juice through sieve into measuring cup, pressing on solids. Discard solids. Chop remaining tomatoes.

5   Stir 1½ cups tomato juice into rice mixture. Re-cover with vented plastic wrap; microwave on Medium for 5 minutes or until most liquid is absorbed.

6   Stir corn into rice mixture, cover again with vented plastic wrap; microwave on Medium for 3 minutes or until corn is heated through.

7   Stir Parmesan, green beans, chopped tomatoes, salt, pepper, and half of basil into risotto. Sprinkle with remaining basil before serving.

390 CALORIES

PER SERVING. 12G PROTEIN | 70G CARBOHYDRATE | 8G TOTAL FAT (5G SATURATED) 6G FIBER | 8MG CHOLESTEROL | 485MG SODIUM ❂

MAKE IT A MEAL: Serve with Sliced Citrus with Lime Syrup (95 calories; page 140). In summer, make the syrup and use on unpeeled nectarines or peaches.

330 CALORIES

California Breakfast Wrap
(page 91)

BREAKFAST AROUND THE CLOCK

You've heard it before, and we'll say it again: A good breakfast is the foundation of any healthy diet. So why not enjoy the light and healthy vegetarian breakfasts that follow morning, noon, or night? Our egg-based frittatas, tarts, wraps, and scrambles are not only perfect for brunch; they make stellar vegetarian dinners, too. (See "The Nutritional Benefits of Eggs" on page 97). If you're hankering for something sweet, you can tuck into our pancakes and French toast without guilt because they're prepared with whole grains. Or, for something different, sample our savory take on pancakes; they are enriched with a little reduced-fat ricotta and topped with a delectable tomato and Swiss chard sauce.

KEY TO ICONS

⬤ 30 minutes or less   Ⓥ Vegan   ♥ Heart healthy   ✹ High fiber   ▬ Make ahead

FIVE-MINUTE MULTIGRAIN CEREAL

Get a great-grains start to your day with a hot and tasty serving of three kinds of grains—it cooks up in five minutes flat. Serve it with your choice of low-fat or nondairy milk.

ACTIVE TIME: 5 MINUTES · **TOTAL TIME:** 10 MINUTES
MAKES: 1 SERVING

2 TABLESPOONS QUICK-COOKING BARLEY	2 TABLESPOONS DARK SEEDLESS RAISINS
2 TABLESPOONS BULGUR	PINCH GROUND CINNAMON
2 TABLESPOONS OLD-FASHIONED OATS, UNCOOKED	1 TABLESPOON CHOPPED WALNUTS OR PECANS
⅔ CUP WATER	

In microwave-safe 1-quart bowl, combine barley, bulgur, oats, and water. Microwave on High for 2 minutes. Stir in raisins and cinnamon; microwave 3 minutes longer. Stir, then top with walnuts.

265 CALORIES

PER SERVING. 8G PROTEIN | 50G CARBOHYDRATE | 6G TOTAL FAT (1G SATURATED) 7G FIBER | 0MG CHOLESTEROL | 5MG SODIUM 🟢 Ⓥ ❤️ 🌱

MAKE IT A MEAL: For a wholesome start to your day, pour on ½ cup low-fat (2%) milk or soy milk (60 or 65 calories). If you want to add some protein to keep you going, serve with one hard-boiled egg (80 calories).

SCRAMBLED EGGS WITH FRESH HERBS

Scrambled eggs are the perfect quick and easy protein-filled dish to start your morning off right. The Dijon mustard and herbs add flavor, so there's no need to add cheese.

TOTAL TIME: 10 MINUTES

MAKES: 4 MAIN-DISH SERVINGS

8   LARGE EGGS, BEATEN

2   TABLESPOONS BUTTER OR MARGARINE

⅛   TEASPOON SALT

⅛   TEASPOON GROUND BLACK PEPPER

1½ TEASPOONS DIJON MUSTARD

¼   CUP PACKED FRESH FLAT-LEAF PARSLEY LEAVES, FINELY CHOPPED, PLUS ADDITIONAL FOR GARNISH

¼   CUP FINELY CHOPPED FRESH CHIVES, PLUS ADDITIONAL WHOLE CHIVES FOR GARNISH

1 In 12-inch skillet, combine eggs, butter, salt, and pepper. Turn heat to medium-low. With wire whisk, gently and constantly whisk 3 to 5 minutes or until soft curds form but eggs are still wet.

2 Whisk in Dijon mustard, then chopped parsley and chives. Continue whisking 1 to 2 minutes or until eggs are almost set and very creamy. Immediately remove skillet from heat and spoon eggs into warmed large serving bowl. Garnish with additional herbs.

205 **CALORIES** **PER SERVING.** 13G PROTEIN | 2G CARBOHYDRATE | 16G TOTAL FAT (4G SATURATED) 0G FIBER | 425MG CHOLESTEROL | 285MG SODIUM ⌄

MAKE IT A MEAL: The possibilities are endless: Keep it simple and add on a slice of toast spread with 1 teaspoon trans-fat-free margarine (115 calories). Or serve the eggs with a Whole-Grain Blueberry Muffin (170 calories; page 134) and ½ grapefruit (40 calories); it's just 415 calories for the whole meal.

CALIFORNIA BREAKFAST WRAP

Filling and filled with good-for-you-ingredients, this wrap is the perfect way to start your morning. It's packed with protein from the eggs and cheese, healthy fats from the avocado, and cancer-fighting antioxidants and lycopene from the spinach and tomato. For photo, see page 86.

TOTAL TIME: 25 MINUTES

MAKES: 4 MAIN-DISH SERVINGS

---

4 LARGE EGGS	1 TEASPOON CANOLA OIL
2 LARGE EGG WHITES	1 RIPE MEDIUM TOMATO, SEEDED AND FINELY CHOPPED (1 CUP)
⅜ TEASPOON SALT	
⅛ TEASPOON GROUND BLACK PEPPER	1 HASS AVOCADO, FINELY CHOPPED
4 (8-INCH) WHOLE-WHEAT TORTILLAS	1 TABLESPOON CHOPPED FRESH DILL LEAVES
4 TABLESPOONS GOAT CHEESE	
3½ OUNCES BABY SPINACH (7 CUPS)	

1 In medium bowl, beat eggs, egg whites, and ⅛ teaspoon each salt and pepper.

2 On microwave-safe plate, cover tortillas with damp paper towel. Microwave on High for 30 seconds or until just warm and pliable.

3 Spread 1 tablespoon goat cheese on each tortilla; divide spinach evenly on top of cheese.

4 In 12-inch nonstick skillet, heat oil over medium heat. Add egg mixture. Cook 2 minutes or until almost set, stirring gently. Remove from heat; fold in tomato, avocado, and remaining ¼ teaspoon salt.

5 Divide hot egg mixture among tortillas. Top with dill; fold in half.

330 CALORIES

PER SERVING. 16G PROTEIN | 29G CARBOHYDRATE | 16G TOTAL FAT (4G SATURATED) 6G FIBER | 191MG CHOLESTEROL | 565MG SODIUM ●

MAKE IT A MEAL: You don't need more than a fruit salad to complete this meal: Pair it with ½ cup cubed melon and 1 sliced kiwi fruit per person to create a 395-calorie breakfast or brunch.

TOSTADA STACKS

Try this new spin on tostadas served with a tomato-zucchini salsa and fried eggs on top. It's a hit at brunches.

ACTIVE TIME: 30 MINUTES · **TOTAL TIME:** 35 MINUTES
MAKES: 4 MAIN-DISH SERVINGS

- 4 (6-INCH) CORN TORTILLAS
- 4 TEASPOONS VEGETABLE OIL
- 1 MEDIUM WHITE ONION, FINELY CHOPPED
- 3 GARLIC CLOVES, CHOPPED
- ¾ TEASPOON SALT
- ¼ TEASPOON GROUND BLACK PEPPER
- 1 CAN (15 TO 19 OUNCES) LOW-SODIUM BLACK BEANS, RINSED AND DRAINED
- 1 MEDIUM ZUCCHINI (8 OUNCES), FINELY CHOPPED
- 1 MEDIUM ORANGE PEPPER, FINELY CHOPPED
- 2 CUPS FRESH CORN KERNELS
- 2 RIPE PLUM TOMATOES, FINELY CHOPPED
- 1 TEASPOON CHIPOTLE HOT SAUCE
- 2 TABLESPOONS FRESH LIME JUICE
- 2 TABLESPOONS CHOPPED FRESH CILANTRO
- 4 LARGE EGGS

1 Place tortillas between two paper towels on large plate. Microwave on High for 3 minutes or until crisp.

2 In nonstick 12-inch skillet, heat 1 tablespoon oil over medium heat. Add onion, garlic, and ⅛ teaspoon each salt and pepper. Cook 8 minutes or until golden, stirring.

3 Meanwhile, place beans and ¼ teaspoon salt in medium bowl. In large bowl, combine zucchini, orange pepper, corn, tomatoes, hot sauce, lime juice, 1 tablespoon cilantro, and ¼ teaspoon salt. Add half of onion mixture to beans; mash well. Stir remaining onion mixture into vegetables.

4 Wipe pan. Heat remaining 1 teaspoon oil over medium heat. Fry eggs 6 minutes or until whites are set. Sprinkle with remaining ⅛ teaspoon salt.

5 Meanwhile, spread bean mixture on tortillas. Top each with fried egg; serve with zucchini mix. Sprinkle with remaining 1 tablespoon cilantro.

375 **CALORIES**

PER SERVING. 19G PROTEIN | 53G CARBOHYDRATE | 11G TOTAL FAT (2G SATURATED) 10G FIBER | 186MG CHOLESTEROL | 605MG SODIUM

MAKE IT A MEAL: This brunch favorite can stand on its own. But if you want, serve with ½ cup frozen grapes (50 calories) to make it a 425-calorie meal.

CRUSTLESS TOMATO-RICOTTA PIE

This delicious cross between a frittata and a quiche makes a great vegetarian dinner or brunch option. Try this simple cheese-and-tomato pie with 2 tablespoons chopped fresh oregano or ¼ cup chopped fresh dill in place of the basil.

ACTIVE TIME: 20 MINUTES · **TOTAL TIME:** 55 MINUTES PLUS STANDING
MAKES: 4 MAIN-DISH SERVINGS

1 CONTAINER (15 OUNCES) PART-SKIM RICOTTA CHEESE	1 TABLESPOON CORNSTARCH
4 LARGE EGGS	½ CUP LOOSELY PACKED FRESH BASIL LEAVES, CHOPPED
¼ CUP FRESHLY GRATED PECORINO ROMANO CHEESE	½ CUP LOOSELY PACKED FRESH MINT LEAVES, CHOPPED
½ TEASPOON SALT	1 POUND RIPE TOMATOES, THINLY SLICED
⅛ TEASPOON COARSELY GROUND BLACK PEPPER	
¼ CUP LOW-FAT MILK (1%)	

1 Preheat oven to 375°F. In large bowl, whisk ricotta, eggs, Romano, salt, and pepper until blended.

2 In measuring cup, stir milk and cornstarch until smooth; whisk into cheese mixture. Stir in basil and mint.

3 Pour mixture into 10-inch nonstick skillet with oven-safe handle. Arrange tomato slices on top, overlapping if necessary. Bake pie 35 to 40 minutes or until edge is lightly browned and set and center is puffed. Let stand 5 minutes before serving.

190 CALORIES

PER SERVING. 15G PROTEIN | 10G CARBOHYDRATE | 10G TOTAL FAT (5G SATURATED)
2G FIBER | 165MG CHOLESTEROL | 380MG SODIUM

MAKE IT A MEAL: If you want to serve this for dinner or brunch, pair with Greens with Goat Cheese and Tangerine Vinaigrette (165 calories; page 121) for a 355-calorie meal.

TOMATO TARTE TATIN

Frozen puff pastry is the shortcut secret to this skillet dish.

ACTIVE TIME: 30 MINUTES · **TOTAL TIME:** 1 HOUR PLUS COOLING
MAKES: 6 MAIN-DISH SERVINGS

1   FROZEN SHEET PUFF PASTRY
    (HALF 17⅓-OUNCE PACKAGE), THAWED

1   TABLESPOON OLIVE OIL

1   MEDIUM ONION, CHOPPED

1   LARGE YELLOW PEPPER, CHOPPED

½   TEASPOON SALT

¼   TEASPOON GROUND BLACK PEPPER

1   TEASPOON FRESH THYME

2   TABLESPOONS BUTTER
    (NO SUBSTITUTIONS)

2   TABLESPOONS SUGAR

1½ POUNDS FIRM RIPE PLUM TOMATOES,
    SEEDED, CUT IN HALF LENGTHWISE

3   OUNCES GOAT CHEESE, CRUMBLED

8   SMALL FRESH BASIL LEAVES

1   Preheat oven to 400°F. On lightly floured surface, with floured rolling pin, roll pastry into 12-inch square; cut into 12-inch round. Place on waxed-paper-lined cookie sheet; refrigerate.

2   In 12-inch heavy ovenproof skillet, heat oil over medium heat. Add onion, yellow pepper, and ⅛ teaspoon each salt and pepper. Cook 6 minutes or just until tender, stirring. Stir in thyme; cook 1 minute. Transfer to bowl.

3   To same pan, add butter and sugar; cook 1 to 2 minutes, stirring. Add tomatoes, cut sides down, in single layer; cover, cook 2 minutes, then uncover. Cook 3 to 4 minutes or until most of pan juices are reduced, swirling pan frequently. Turn tomatoes over; sprinkle with ¼ teaspoon salt and ⅛ teaspoon pepper. Cook 2 minutes or until softened, swirling pan frequently; any remaining liquid should be thick and glossy. Remove pan from heat.

4   Sprinkle onion mixture over tomatoes. Carefully invert dough from waxed paper into mixture in pan. Cut six small slits in dough. Bake 30 to 35 minutes or until crust is dark golden brown. Cool in pan 10 minutes.

5   To unmold, place platter over top of tart. Quickly and carefully turn platter with skillet upside down to invert tart; remove skillet. Sprinkle tart with ⅛ teaspoon salt, goat cheese, and basil. Serve immediately.

290 CALORIES

PER SERVING. 7G PROTEIN | 27G CARBOHYDRATE | 18G TOTAL FAT (7G SATURATED) 3G FIBER | 17MG CHOLESTEROL | 440MG SODIUM

MAKE IT A MEAL: Serve with Spring Pea Dip with Veggies (50 calories; page 109) for a delightful 340-calorie brunch.

ASPARAGUS TART

This spring tart is an elegant addition to any brunch table.

ACTIVE TIME: 25 MINUTES · **TOTAL TIME:** 1 HOUR PLUS COOLING
MAKES: 8 MAIN-DISH SERVINGS

1⅜ TEASPOONS SALT

1¾ CUPS ALL-PURPOSE FLOUR

1   TEASPOON BAKING POWDER

¼   TEASPOON GROUND BLACK PEPPER

6   TABLESPOONS COLD BUTTER OR
    MARGARINE, CUT UP

6   TO 8 TABLESPOONS ICE WATER

1   POUND THIN ASPARAGUS, TRIMMED
    (SEE TIP, PAGE 72)

3   LARGE EGGS

1⅓ CUPS MILK

1   TEASPOON DIJON MUSTARD

2   TEASPOONS GRATED FRESH
    LEMON PEEL

1 Preheat oven to 425°F. In covered 10-inch skillet over high heat, bring about 1 *inch water* and 1 teaspoon salt to boiling. Spray removable bottom of 11-inch tart pan with cooking spray.

2 In food processor with knife blade attached, combine flour, baking powder, ⅛ teaspoon salt, and ¼ teaspoon pepper; pulse until blended. Add butter and pulse until mixture resembles coarse meal. Add ice water, 1 tablespoon at a time, pulsing until moist clumps form. Gather dough together and flatten into disk. On lightly floured surface, with floured rolling pin, roll dough into 13-inch round. Gently ease dough into prepared tart pan. Fold overhang inward and press against dough on side of pan to reinforce edge (dough can be covered and refrigerated up to 4 hours before baking). Place pan on cookie sheet; bake 15 minutes. Cool slightly on wire rack.

3 Meanwhile, add asparagus to boiling water in skillet and cook 5 minutes. Drain and rinse under cold running water; drain well. In medium bowl, with wire whisk or fork, mix eggs, milk, Dijon, and remaining ¼ teaspoon salt until well blended.

THE NUTRITIONAL BENEFITS OF EGGS

Eggs got a bum rap for years. Yes, the yolk of an egg does contain cholesterol, but as hundreds of studies can attest, if eaten in moderation, eggs won't raise a person's overall cholesterol level. And eggs have so much to offer nutritionally. A single egg is a good source of selenium, which provides antioxidant protection; iodine, vital to thyroid function; energy-producing vitamin B_2; and protein.

4 Arrange asparagus spears in spoke fashion in baked tart shell with tips pointing outward. Sprinkle lemon peel evenly over asparagus in tart shell. Carefully pour egg mixture over asparagus.

5 Bake tart, on cookie sheet, 20 to 25 minutes or until tart puffs and custard jiggles only slightly in center. Cool on wire rack 15 minutes to serve warm or cool completely to serve at room temperature. Remove side of pan before serving.

245 **PER SERVING.** 8G PROTEIN | 24G CARBOHYDRATE | 13G TOTAL FAT (7G SATURATED)
CALORIES 1G FIBER | 110MG CHOLESTEROL | 340MG SODIUM

MAKE IT A MEAL: To create a memorable brunch spread, add a basket of our Bran Muffins (140 calories; page 127) and a bowl of fresh strawberries, halved (25 calories for ½ cup). A slice of Asparagus Tart, a muffin, and one serving strawberries comes in at just 410 calories.

SOUTHWESTERN FRITTATA

Frittatas are a great choice for breakfast, brunch, or a light dinner.

ACTIVE TIME: 25 MINUTES · **TOTAL TIME:** 50 MINUTES PLUS STANDING
MAKES: 6 MAIN-DISH SERVINGS

---

1 PACKAGE (8 TO 9 OUNCES) PRECOOKED BROWN RICE (SCANT 2 CUPS)

4 TEASPOONS OLIVE OIL

1 SMALL ONION, CHOPPED

1 JALAPEÑO CHILE, SEEDED AND FINELY CHOPPED

1 GARLIC CLOVE, FINELY CHOPPED

1 CUP FROZEN CORN KERNELS

8 LARGE EGGS

¼ CUP MILK

¼ CUP LOOSELY PACKED FRESH CILANTRO LEAVES, CHOPPED

½ TEASPOON SALT

½ CUP SHREDDED MEXICAN CHEESE BLEND

PREPARED SALSA (OPTIONAL)

1 Prepare brown rice as label directs. Preheat oven to 400°F.

2 In nonstick 10-inch skillet with oven-safe handle, heat 2 teaspoons olive oil over medium-high heat until hot. Add onion and cook until lightly browned, 2 to 3 minutes, stirring occasionally. Stir in jalapeño and garlic; cook 30 seconds, stirring. Add frozen corn and cook until thawed, about 1 minute, stirring a few times. Transfer corn mixture to bowl.

3 In large bowl, with wire whisk, beat eggs, milk, cilantro, and salt until well blended. Stir in rice, corn mixture, and cheese.

4 In same skillet, heat remaining 2 teaspoons oil over medium heat until hot. Pour in egg mixture; cover and cook until egg mixture starts to set around edge, about 3 minutes.

5 Remove cover and place skillet in oven; bake until knife inserted 2 inches from edge comes out clean, about 20 minutes. Remove frittata from oven; let stand 5 minutes.

6 To serve, loosen frittata from skillet; slide onto warm platter. Cut into wedges; serve with salsa if you like.

---

245 CALORIES

PER SERVING. 13G PROTEIN | 19G CARBOHYDRATE | 14G TOTAL FAT (5G SATURATED) 2G FIBER | 293MG CHOLESTEROL | 355MG SODIUM

MAKE IT A MEAL: For a fun 390-calorie meal, pair this mildly spicy frittata with our cooling Banana Berry Parfait (145 calories; page 143).

CHILES RELLEÑOS CASSEROLE

Green chiles and Cheddar cheese are baked into eggs for a healthy take on a classic dish.

ACTIVE TIME: 15 MINUTES · **TOTAL TIME:** 50 MINUTES PLUS COOLING
MAKES: 4 MAIN-DISH SERVINGS

- 6 LARGE EGGS
- 1 CUP REDUCED-FAT MILK (2%)
- 2 TABLESPOONS ALL-PURPOSE FLOUR
- ¼ TEASPOON SWEET PAPRIKA
- ¼ TEASPOON SALT
- ½ TEASPOON GROUND BLACK PEPPER
- 2 CANS (5¾ OUNCES EACH) WHOLE GREEN CHILES, DRAINED AND THINLY SLICED

- 1 LARGE RED PEPPER, CUT INTO ¼-INCH PIECES
- 4 OUNCES EXTRA-SHARP CHEDDAR CHEESE, SHREDDED (1 CUP)
- ½ CUP PACKED FRESH CILANTRO LEAVES, FINELY CHOPPED

1 Preheat oven to 350°F. Grease shallow 2-quart ceramic or glass baking dish well.

2 In large bowl, with wire whisk, mix eggs, milk, flour, paprika, salt, and black pepper until well blended. Stir in chiles, red pepper, Cheddar, and half of cilantro; pour into prepared dish.

3 Bake casserole 35 to 40 minutes or until surface is puffed and golden brown and center still jiggles slightly.

4 Cool in dish on wire rack 10 minutes. Garnish with remaining chopped cilantro and cut into squares or wedges to serve.

305 CALORIES

PER SERVING. 20G PROTEIN | 14G CARBOHYDRATE | 18G TOTAL FAT (9G SATURATED) 3G FIBER | 353MG CHOLESTEROL | 825MG SODIUM

MAKE IT A MEAL: This is an egg dish that easily translates to lunch or dinner. Serve with a side of baked tortilla chips (15 chips for 125 calories) and dip them into the casserole for a casual 430-calorie meal your whole family will enjoy.

SAVORY RICOTTA PANCAKES

Pancakes transcend breakfast when they're made with ricotta cheese and topped with an Italian tomato and Swiss chard sauce.

ACTIVE TIME: 55 MINUTES · **TOTAL TIME:** 1 HOUR 10 MINUTES

MAKES: 16 PANCAKES OR 4 MAIN-DISH SERVINGS

- 1 SMALL BUNCH (8 OUNCES) SWISS CHARD, TOUGH ENDS TRIMMED
- 1 TABLESPOON OLIVE OIL
- 1 MEDIUM ONION, CHOPPED
- 1 GARLIC CLOVE, CRUSHED WITH GARLIC PRESS
- 1 TABLESPOON TOMATO PASTE
- 1 CAN (28 OUNCES) WHOLE TOMATOES IN PUREE, CHOPPED
- ½ TEASPOON SALT

- 3 LARGE EGGS, SEPARATED
- 1 CUP PART-SKIM RICOTTA CHEESE
- ⅓ CUP REDUCED-FAT MILK (2%)
- ½ CUP ALL-PURPOSE FLOUR
- ¼ TEASPOON BAKING POWDER
- 1 TABLESPOON BUTTER OR MARGARINE, CUT INTO 3 PIECES
- ¼ CUP FRESHLY GRATED PECORINO ROMANO CHEESE

1 Cut ribs and stems from Swiss chard leaves. Cut ribs and stems into 1-inch pieces; cut leaves into 2-inch pieces. Rinse chard thoroughly in large bowl of cold water; swish to remove any dirt. With hands, transfer chard to colander, leaving dirt in bottom of bowl. Repeat process, changing water until all dirt is removed.

2 In 4-quart saucepan, heat olive oil over medium heat until hot. Add onion and garlic, and cook 6 to 8 minutes or until tender. Add tomato paste; cook 1 minute, stirring. Add tomatoes with their puree and ¼ teaspoon salt; heat to boiling over medium-high heat. Stir in Swiss chard; reduce heat to medium-low and simmer, covered, 10 minutes. Remove cover and cook 8 to 10 minutes longer or until chard is tender and sauce is thickened slightly, stirring occasionally. Remove saucepan from heat; cover to keep sauce warm.

3 Meanwhile, preheat oven to 200°F. In blender or food processor with knife blade attached, blend egg yolks, ricotta, and milk until smooth. Add flour, baking powder, and remaining ¼ teaspoon salt, and blend until smooth; transfer batter to 8-cup glass measure or medium bowl.

4 In small bowl, with mixer on high speed, beat egg whites just until stiff peaks form when beaters are lifted. With rubber spatula, fold beaten whites into batter.

5 In nonstick 12-inch skillet, melt 1 piece butter over medium heat. Drop batter by ¼ cups into skillet, making 4 to 5 pancakes per batch. Cook 3 to 4 minutes or until edges look dry and bottoms are browned. Turn pancakes over and cook 2 to 3 minutes or until bottoms are browned. Transfer pancakes to platter; keep warm in oven.

6 Repeat with remaining butter and batter. Serve pancakes with warm sauce; sprinkle with Romano.

350 CALORIES **PER SERVING.** 19G PROTEIN | 31G CARBOHYDRATE | 17G TOTAL FAT (6G SATURATED) 3G FIBER | 185MG CHOLESTEROL | 1,155MG SODIUM

MAKE IT A MEAL: Pair these savory pancakes with a Morningstar veggie sausage patty to make it a 430-calorie brunch. Or add a small micro-baked apple (55 calories).

TEMPTING PANCAKE TOPPERS

Maple syrup will always be a classic, but here are some other wholesome and delicious topping options.

- Drizzle ¼ cup low-fat vanilla yogurt (50 calories per ¼ cup) over the raspberries and chopped nectarines called for in the recipe.

- Dollop with part-skim ricotta (80 calories for ¼ cup) and fresh orange pieces (40 calories for ¼ cup).

- Spread with 2 tablespoons apple butter or other favorite fruit puree (40 calories) and sprinkle with 1 tablespoon roasted pumpkin seeds (35 calories).

- Drizzle with 1 tablespoon maple syrup (50 calories) and sprinkle with 1 tablespoon toasted chopped pecans (45 calories) plus 1 tablespoon sweetened coconut flakes (30 calories).

WHOLE-GRAIN PANCAKES

Have a stack of pancakes without a side of guilt. These flapjacks contain oats and whole-wheat flour. They're topped with delicious fresh fruit.

TOTAL TIME: 30 MINUTES

MAKES: 12 PANCAKES OR 4 MAIN-DISH SERVINGS

2	RIPE PEACHES, PITTED AND CHOPPED	2	TEASPOONS BAKING POWDER
½	PINT RASPBERRIES (1½ CUPS)	½	TEASPOON SALT
1	TABLESPOON SUGAR	1¼	CUPS SKIM MILK
½	CUP ALL-PURPOSE FLOUR	1	LARGE EGG, LIGHTLY BEATEN
½	CUP WHOLE-WHEAT FLOUR	1	TABLESPOON VEGETABLE OIL
½	CUP QUICK-COOKING OATS, UNCOOKED		

1 Preheat oven to 200°F. In medium bowl, combine peaches, raspberries, and sugar. Stir to coat; set fruit mixture aside.

2 In large bowl, combine flours, oats, baking powder, and salt. Add milk, egg, and oil; stir just until flour mixture is moistened; batter will be lumpy.

3 Spray 12-inch nonstick skillet with cooking spray; heat over medium heat 1 minute. Pour batter by scant ¼ cups into skillet, making about 4 pancakes at a time. Cook until tops are bubbly, some bubbles burst, and edges look dry. With wide spatula, turn pancakes over and cook until undersides are golden. Transfer pancakes to platter. Cover; keep warm in oven.

4 Repeat with remaining batter, using more nonstick cooking spray if necessary. To serve, top with fruit mixture.

275 CALORIES

PER SERVING. 10G PROTEIN | 46G CARBOHYDRATE | 6G TOTAL FAT (1G SATURATED) 6G FIBER | 55MG CHOLESTEROL | 545MG SODIUM

MAKE IT A MEAL: What are pancakes without maple syrup? Add 1 tablespoon to make this a 325-calorie breakfast.

EASY ADD-ONS

To make your meal planning a breeze, we've organized the add-on recipes in the following chapters by calorie count—from lowest to highest. Choose your main dish from the preceding chapters, then select one or more of these tempting veggie or grain sides or desserts to round out your meal. So, if you're preparing our Vegetable Lasagna, a 310-calorie main dish, you could serve Artichokes with Creamy Lemon Sauce (145 calories) as a starter, or you could enjoy two lower-calorie add-ons instead: Mesclun with Pears and Pumpkin Seeds (100 calories) plus Sliced Citrus with Lime Syrup (95 calories) for dessert—and your dinner still adds up to approximately 500 calories total. It's that easy!

50
CALORIES

*Spring Pea Dip
With Veggies
(page 109)*

SNACKS, SIDES & SALADS

For generations, the mealtime mantra of mothers everywhere has been "Eat your vegetables!" As usual, Mom was right. In study after study, it's been shown that eating a diet rich in vegetables, fruits, and whole grains results in numerous health benefits, from reducing the risk of some cancers to maintaining a healthy weight. In this chapter, we provide delicious and original recipes for broccoli and peas, dark greens and artichokes, mixed vegetables and side salads. Add these colorful sides onto your meals—and make your mother proud.

KEY TO ICONS

⏱ 30 minutes or less Ⓥ Vegan ♥ Heart healthy ✺ High fiber ▭ Make ahead

KALE CHIPS

Our crisp kale "chips" are virtually fat free—perfect for guilt-free snacking.

ACTIVE TIME: 10 MINUTES · TOTAL TIME: 20 MINUTES
MAKES: 6 SIDE-DISH SERVINGS

Preheat oven to 350°F. From **1 bunch kale** (10 ounces), remove and discard thick stems, and tear leaves into large pieces. Spread leaves in single layer on two large cookie sheets. Coat leaves lightly with nonstick cooking spray and sprinkle with **½ teaspoon salt**. Bake 12 to 15 minutes or just until crisp but not browned. Cool on cookie sheets on wire racks.

15 CALORIES

PER 1-CUP SERVING. 1G PROTEIN | 3G CARBOHYDRATE | 0G TOTAL FAT | 1G FIBER
0MG CHOLESTEROL | 175MG SODIUM

SAUTÉED SPINACH WITH GARLIC AND LEMON

This lemon-kissed sautéed spinach is packed with folate, iron, calcium, and vitamins A and C.

ACTIVE TIME: 5 MINUTES · TOTAL TIME: 10 MINUTES
MAKES: 4 SIDE-DISH SERVINGS

In 6-quart saucepot, heat **1 tablespoon olive oil** over medium-high heat. Add **2 crushed garlic cloves** and cook 1 minute or until golden, stirring. Rinse **2 bags (10 ounces each) spinach** and add to pot, with water still clinging to leaves, in 3 batches; cook 2 minutes or until spinach fits in pot. Cover and cook 2 minutes longer or just until spinach wilts, stirring once. Stir in **1 tablespoon lemon juice** and ¼ **teaspoon salt** and serve.

45 CALORIES

PER SERVING. 4G PROTEIN | 1G CARBOHYDRATE | 4G TOTAL FAT (1G SATURATED) 12G FIBER | 0MG CHOLESTEROL | 305MG SODIUM

SPRING PEA DIP

Serve this vibrant green dip with assorted spring vegetables for dipping, such as cucumber strips, yellow and red pepper strips, and baby carrots, or with homemade pita chips. For photo, see page 106.

ACTIVE TIME: 15 MINUTES · TOTAL TIME: 20 MINUTES
MAKES: 1 CUP

In food processor with knife blade attached, puree **1 cup thawed frozen peas,** with ¼ **cup loosely packed mint leaves,** chopped; and ¼ **teaspoon each salt and pepper.** Transfer to small bowl; stir in ⅓ **cup part-skim ricotta cheese** and **2 tablespoons freshly grated Parmesan cheese.** Serve dip, with ½ **cup assorted raw vegetables**, or cover and refrigerate to serve later.

50 CALORIES

PER SERVING. 4G PROTEIN | 7G CARBOHYDRATE | 1G TOTAL FAT (1G SATURATED) 2G FIBER | 4MG CHOLESTEROL | 120MG SODIUM

SHREDDED BEETS WITH CELERY AND DATES

This simple salad features raw grated beets, which lend the salad high crunch appeal and showcase the rich, earthy flavor of beets.

TOTAL TIME: 10 MINUTES

MAKES: 4 CUPS OR 8 SIDE-DISH SERVINGS

Cut **1 pound peeled beets** into quarters. In food processor with shredding blade attached, shred beets; transfer to large bowl. Stir in **3 stalks thinly sliced celery, ½ cup chopped pitted dates, 3 tablespoons fresh lemon juice,** and **¼ teaspoon each salt and coarsely ground black pepper.** If not serving right away, cover and refrigerate up to 4 hours.

50 CALORIES

PER SERVING. 1G PROTEIN | 13G CARBOHYDRATE | 0G TOTAL FAT | 2G FIBER | 0MG CHOLESTEROL | 110MG SODIUM ♥ ♥ ♥ ▄

ROASTED CAULIFLOWER

Our favorite way to cook cauliflower, roasting delivers a full-flavored, low-fat side dish. Try it with broccoli and halved Brussels Sprouts, too.

ACTIVE TIME: 10 MINUTES · TOTAL TIME: 40 MINUTES

MAKES: 3 CUPS OR 4 SIDE-DISH SERVINGS

Preheat oven to 450°F. **Trim 1 head cauliflower (2 pounds),** separate into 1-inch flowerets, and place in large bowl. Toss with **1 coarsely chopped medium onion, 2 tablespoons reduced-sodium soy sauce, 1 tablespoon olive oil,** and **1 crushed garlic clove** until evenly mixed. Spread mixture in 15½" by 10½" jelly-roll pan. Roast 30 to 35 minutes or until tender and browned, stirring occasionally. Spoon cauliflower into serving bowl; garnish with **snipped fresh chives.**

70 CALORIES

PER SERVING. 3G PROTEIN | 7G CARBOHYDRATE | 4G TOTAL FAT (1G SATURATED) 3G FIBER | 0MG CHOLESTEROL | 300MG SODIUM ♥ ♥

VEGETABLES WITH SESAME VINAIGRETTE

This lively mix of green vegetables, cooked just until crisp-tender and tossed with the rich roasted flavor of sesame oil, will have you and your family eating your vegetables every chance you get.

ACTIVE TIME: 25 MINUTES · TOTAL TIME: 30 MINUTES

MAKES: MAKES 10 SIDE-DISH SERVINGS

1 MEDIUM BUNCH BROCCOLI, CUT INTO 2½-INCH PIECES

2 TABLESPOONS OLIVE OR VEGETABLE OIL

2 MEDIUM ZUCCHINI (8 OUNCES EACH), CUT INTO 1½-INCH CHUNKS

1 BUNCH GREEN ONIONS, CUT INTO 1-INCH PIECES

1½ TEASPOONS SALT

1 POUND ASPARAGUS, TRIMMED AND CUT INTO 2-INCH PIECES

8 OUNCES SUGAR SNAP PEAS OR SNOW PEAS, STEMS AND STRINGS ALONG BOTH EDGES REMOVED

3 TABLESPOONS SEASONED RICE VINEGAR

1 TABLESPOON ASIAN SESAME OIL

½ TEASPOON SUGAR

1 In 3-quart saucepan over high heat, bring 1 inch *water* to boil. Add broccoli and return to boiling. Reduce heat to low; cover and simmer until broccoli is just tender-crisp, 4 to 5 minutes. Drain.

2 In nonstick 12-inch skillet, place 1 tablespoon olive oil over medium-high heat, until hot. Add zucchini, green onions, and ¼ teaspoon salt and cook until vegetables are golden and tender-crisp, stirring frequently; with slotted spoon, remove to bowl.

3 Add remaining 1 tablespoon olive oil to skillet and heat until hot. Add asparagus, snap peas, and ¼ teaspoon salt and cook until vegetables are golden and tender-crisp, stirring frequently.

4 In cup, mix vinegar, sesame oil, sugar, and remaining 1 teaspoon salt. Add zucchini, green onions, and broccoli to vegetables in skillet. Stir in sesame vinaigrette, tossing to coat vegetables well; heat through. Serve warm. Or cover and refrigerate to serve cold later.

80

CALORIES

PER SERVING. 3G PROTEIN | 10G CARBOHYDRATE | 4G TOTAL FAT (0G SATURATED) 3G FIBER | 0MG CHOLESTEROL | 465MG SODIUM ◔ ◉ 🍽

GREEN BEANS WITH MIXED MUSHROOMS

This simple side borrows the basic flavors of a casserole, but features the grabbed-from-the-garden goodness of field-picked beans, thin-sliced onions, and earthy creminis and shiitakes.

ACTIVE TIME: 30 MINUTES · TOTAL TIME: 45 MINUTES
MAKES: 6 SIDE-DISH SERVINGS

1 TABLESPOON OLIVE OIL

2 SPRIGS FRESH THYME

1 LARGE ONION (12 OUNCES), THINLY SLICED

1 GARLIC CLOVE, CRUSHED WITH GARLIC PRESS

4 OUNCES CREMINI MUSHROOMS, THINLY SLICED

4 OUNCES SHIITAKE MUSHROOMS, STEMS DISCARDED, THINLY SLICED

1¼ TEASPOONS SALT

¼ TEASPOON GROUND BLACK PEPPER

1½ POUNDS GREEN BEANS, TRIMMED

1 Heat covered 5- to 6-quart saucepot of *water* to boiling over high heat.

2 Meanwhile, in 12-inch skillet, heat oil over medium-high heat. Add thyme and onion; cook 10 to 12 minutes or until browned and very tender, stirring occasionally. Stir in garlic and cook 1 minute. Add all mushrooms and cook 5 minutes or until tender, stirring occasionally. Stir in ¼ teaspoon each salt and pepper. Remove and discard thyme.

3 Add green beans and remaining 1 teaspoon salt to boiling water. Cook, uncovered, 8 to 9 minutes or until tender, stirring occasionally. Drain and rinse with cold water. If making ahead, transfer mushroom mixture to medium bowl. Cover; refrigerate up to overnight. Transfer beans to zip-tight plastic bag; refrigerate up to overnight.

4 When ready to serve, return green beans to saucepot and add mushroom mixture, stirring to combine. Cook over medium heat until beans are heated through, stirring occasionally.

80
CALORIES

PER SERVING. 3G PROTEIN | 14G CARBOHYDRATE | 3G TOTAL FAT (0G SATURATED)
4G FIBER | 0MG CHOLESTEROL | 125MG SODIUM ◉ ◉ ♥ ▭

MESCLUN WITH PEARS AND PUMPKIN SEEDS

We love slicing pears into autumn salads: The fruit's honeyed juiciness partners perfectly with greens. Instead of the more classic pecans, here we've swapped in toasted pumpkin seeds, or pepitas, which have become a supermarket staple in recent years.

TOTAL TIME: 10 MINUTES

MAKES: 6 SIDE-DISH SERVINGS

2   TABLESPOONS PUMPKIN SEEDS (PEPITAS)

1½ TABLESPOONS APPLE CIDER VINEGAR

½   TABLESPOON DIJON MUSTARD

1   TEASPOON HONEY OR AGAVE NECTAR (SEE TIP)

2   TABLESPOONS EXTRA-VIRGIN OLIVE OIL

2   RIPE RED PEARS, CORED AND THINLY SLICED

1   PACKAGE (5 OUNCES) MIXED BABY GREENS

⅛   TEASPOON SALT

⅛   TEASPOON GROUND BLACK PEPPER

1   In skillet, heat pumpkin seeds over medium heat 2 to 3 minutes or until all are toasted and some start to pop. Cool completely. Toasted seeds can be stored in airtight container up to 1 week.

2   In small bowl, with wire whisk, combine vinegar, Dijon, and honey until blended. Continue whisking and add oil in slow, steady stream. Whisk until well blended and emulsified. Dressing can be made ahead; cover tightly and refrigerate up to 3 days.

3   In large bowl, combine sliced pears, greens, pumpkin seeds, dressing, salt, and pepper. Toss until evenly coated (see Tip).

TIP Agave nectar is a delicious vegan sweetener derived from the agave, a desert plant. You can combine the dressing and pears up to 1 hour before serving to prevent the pears from turning brown. When you're ready to serve, toss in the greens, pumpkin seeds, and seasonings.

100 CALORIES

PER SERVING. 1G PROTEIN | 9G CARBOHYDRATE | 7G TOTAL FAT (1G SATURATED) 2G FIBER | 0MG CHOLESTEROL | 85MG SODIUM ♥ ♥ ♥ ▤

ROOT VEGETABLE GRATIN

Potatoes and vegetables fuse together and can be served as a satisfying meal or side dish in this recipe. This is delicious left over, but you also can easily cut the recipe in half.

ACTIVE TIME: 35 MINUTES · **TOTAL TIME:** 2 HOURS PLUS STANDING
MAKES: 16 SIDE-DISH SERVINGS

¾ CUP CANNED OR HOMEMADE VEGETABLE BROTH (PAGE 37)	1 POUND CELERY ROOT (1 LARGE OR 2 SMALL), TRIMMED, PEELED, QUARTERED, AND THINLY SLICED
2 TABLESPOONS BUTTER OR MARGARINE	1 POUND PARSNIPS (6 MEDIUM), PEELED AND THINLY SLICED
1½ POUNDS RUSSET (BAKING) POTATOES (3 MEDIUM), PEELED AND THINLY SLICED	1¼ TEASPOONS SALT
	½ TEASPOON GROUND BLACK PEPPER
1½ POUNDS SWEET POTATOES (3 SMALL), PEELED AND THINLY SLICED	1 CUP HEAVY OR WHIPPING CREAM
	2 TABLESPOONS SNIPPED FRESH CHIVES

1   Preheat oven to 400°F. In shallow 3½- to 4-quart baking pan or casserole, combine broth and butter; place in oven during preheating to melt butter, about 5 minutes.

2   Meanwhile, in large bowl, toss all potatoes, celery root, and parsnips with salt and pepper until well mixed.

3   Remove baking pan from oven. Add broth mixture to vegetables and stir to coat. Spoon vegetable mixture into baking pan; cover with foil and bake 40 minutes.

4   In 1-cup liquid measuring cup, warm cream in microwave on High for 45 seconds. Pour cream evenly over vegetables. (If making ahead, see Tip.)

5   Return baking pan to oven and bake, uncovered, 30 to 35 minutes longer or until top is golden and vegetables are fork-tender. Let stand 10 minutes, then sprinkle with chives to serve.

TIP To make the gratin ahead, prepare and bake the recipe through step 4; refrigerate it for up to two days. When you're ready to continue, bake it, uncovered, as described in step 5, on the bottom rack of the oven, increasing the final baking time to 55 minutes. Snip the chives for garnish a day ahead and store them in the fridge in plastic wrap.

145 CALORIES **PER SERVING.** 2G PROTEIN | 19G CARBOHYDRATE | 7G TOTAL FAT (4G SATURATED) 3G FIBER | 21MG CHOLESTEROL | 255MG SODIUM ♥

ARTICHOKES WITH CREAMY LEMON SAUCE

Artichokes and lemon are a classic combination—enjoy them in this light and easy side dish.

ACTIVE TIME: 10 MINUTES · TOTAL TIME: 45 MINUTES

MAKES: 4 SIDE-DISH SERVINGS

Fill 6-quart saucepot with 1 *inch water* and place steamer insert in pot. Heat to boiling over high heat; reduce heat to medium. Place **4 artichokes,** stems trimmed, stem side down in saucepot. Cover and steam 35 minutes or until knife pierces easily through base. Stir together ⅓ **cup each light mayonnaise and plain low-fat yogurt, ¼ cup snipped chives, 2 tablespoons each lemon juice and water, 1 tablespoon Dijon mustard,** and **¼ teaspoon salt.** Serve artichokes with sauce.

145 CALORIES

PER SERVING. 5G PROTEIN | 19G CARBOHYDRATE | 7G TOTAL FAT (1G SATURATED) 10G FIBER | 8MG CHOLESTEROL | 475MG SODIUM

CRUNCHY PEANUT BROCCOLI

This dish takes simple steamed broccoli to a gourmet level.

ACTIVE TIME: 20 MINUTES · TOTAL TIME: 30 MINUTES
MAKES: 4 SIDE-DISH SERVINGS

Heat large covered saucepot of **water** to boiling. Fill large bowl with **ice and water.** Add **1 teaspoon salt,** then **1 pound broccoli flowerets,** to boiling water. Cook uncovered 3 to 4 minutes or until crisp-tender. Drain and transfer to ice water. When cool, drain well and place between paper towels to dry. Broccoli can be refrigerated in airtight container up to overnight.

In 12-inch skillet, combine **2 tablespoons vegetable oil** and ¼ **cup chopped roasted unsalted peanuts.** Cook over medium heat 4 minutes or until nuts are golden, stirring occasionally. Stir in **1 small chopped shallot** and cook 1 minute. Stir in **1 teaspoon reduced-sodium soy sauce,** then broccoli. Sprinkle with ¼ **teaspoon each salt and ground black pepper.** Cook 2 minutes or until broccoli is heated through and evenly coated with nut mixture, stirring and tossing. Garnish with the thinly sliced green parts of **1 green onion.**

PER SERVING. 6G PROTEIN | 9G CARBOHYDRATE | 12G TOTAL FAT (1G SATURATED) 4G FIBER | 0MG CHOLESTEROL | 300MG SODIUM 🌿 Ⓥ ♥ 🍴

150 CALORIES

HEALTHY MAKEOVER POTATO SALAD

Our healthy take on classic potato salad just might become your favorite summertime-picnic recipe. This slimmed-down salad (minus 50 calories and 7 fat grams per serving) has just the right level of tangy flavor and no gloppiness. We used light mayo (and less of it than in our traditional recipe) and swapped whole milk with low-fat buttermilk to keep it moist.

ACTIVE TIME: 10 MINUTES · TOTAL TIME: 35 MINUTES PLUS CHILLING
MAKES: 6 CUPS OR 10 SIDE-DISH SERVINGS

3   POUNDS YUKON GOLD POTATOES, PEELED AND CUT INTO 1-INCH CHUNKS

1¼ TEASPOONS SALT

¾   CUP BUTTERMILK

¼   CUP LIGHT MAYONNAISE

2   TABLESPOONS SNIPPED FRESH DILL

2   TABLESPOONS CIDER VINEGAR

1   TABLESPOON DIJON MUSTARD

2   GREEN ONIONS, THINLY SLICED

¼   TEASPOON COARSELY GROUND BLACK PEPPER

1   In 4-quart saucepan, combine potatoes, 1 teaspoon salt, and enough *water to cover*; heat to boiling over high heat. Reduce heat to medium-low; cover and simmer 10 minutes or until potatoes are just fork-tender.

2   Meanwhile, in large bowl, whisk buttermilk with mayonnaise, dill, vinegar, Dijon, green onions, remaining ¼ teaspoon salt, and pepper.

3   Drain potatoes well. Toss hot potatoes with buttermilk dressing until coated; mixture will look very loose before chilling. Cover and refrigerate potato salad at least 2 hours or overnight to blend flavors and cool slightly, stirring gently after 1 hour.

150 CALORIES

PER SERVING. 3G PROTEIN | 29G CARBOHYDRATE | 2G TOTAL FAT (0G SATURATED) 2G FIBER | 3MG CHOLESTEROL | 200MG SODIUM ♥ 🛒

GREENS WITH GOAT CHEESE AND TANGERINE VINAIGRETTE

Savory goat cheese is the perfect companion to our sweet and tangy citrus vinaigrette. If you crave something other than raisins as a garnish, try dried cranberries or apricots.

TOTAL TIME: 15 MINUTES

MAKES: 4 SIDE-DISH SERVINGS

2   TANGERINES

2   TEASPOONS CIDER VINEGAR

½   TEASPOON DIJON MUSTARD

¼   TEASPOON SALT

⅛   TEASPOON GROUND BLACK PEPPER

2   TABLESPOONS OLIVE OIL

1   TABLESPOON CHOPPED FRESH CHIVES

8   CUPS LOOSELY PACKED MIXED BABY GREENS SUCH AS ROMAINE, ARUGULA, AND/OR SPINACH

½   CUP CRUMBLED GOAT CHEESE (2 OUNCES)

¼   CUP GOLDEN RAISINS

1   From tangerines, grate 1 teaspoon peel; place in small bowl. Cut remaining peel and pith from fruit. Hold tangerine over second small bowl and cut on either side of membranes to remove each segment, allowing fruit and juice to drop into bowl. Repeat with remaining tangerine. Squeeze 3 tablespoons juice from membranes; add to bowl with peel, then whisk in vinegar, Dijon, salt, and pepper. In thin, steady stream, whisk in oil until vinaigrette is blended. Stir in tangerine segments and chives.

2   Place greens on salad plates; sprinkle each with goat cheese and raisins. Drizzle with vinaigrette.

165 CALORIES

PER SERVING. 3G PROTEIN | 15G CARBOHYDRATE | 10G TOTAL FAT (3G SATURATED) 2G FIBER | 10MG CHOLESTEROL | 335MG SODIUM ♡ ♥

185 CALORIES

Peach, Cucumber, and Barley Salad (page 128)

GET YOUR GRAINS

We've all heard about the health benefits of whole grains—how eating three servings a day of these "good carbs" can reduce our chances of stroke, heart disease, and type 2 diabetes. But if you're unsure how to incorporate their heart-healthy goodness into your daily meals, we provide plenty of easy, delicious possibilities. From salads featuring barley, wheat-berries, and bulgur to cornbread, whole-wheat biscuits, and two kinds of whole-grain muffins, these sides will help ensure that you and your family get your daily grains. To familiarize yourself with the many whole grains now available in most supermarkets, see "The Vegetarian Pantry" on page 12 for a glossary of grains.

KEY TO ICONS

⌄ 30 minutes or less   Ⓥ Vegan   ♥ Heart healthy   ❀ High fiber   ▭ Make ahead

DOUBLE CORNBREAD

Adding whole corn kernels enhances the texture and flavor of hearty cornbread, which is a terrific item to make ahead. You can freeze the baked cornbread, tightly wrapped, for up to 1 month. When you're ready to serve it, thaw it completely, then reheat it, covered, at 450°F for 15 minutes—it'll come out tasting as fresh as the day you first made it.

ACTIVE TIME: 20 MINUTES · TOTAL TIME: 40 MINUTES
MAKES: 24 SIDE-DISH SERVINGS

1½ CUPS ALL-PURPOSE FLOUR

1½ CUPS YELLOW CORNMEAL

¼ CUP SUGAR

4 TEASPOONS BAKING POWDER

½ TEASPOON BAKING SODA

1 TEASPOON SALT

2½ CUPS BUTTERMILK

3 LARGE EGGS

1 PACKAGE (10 OUNCES) FROZEN CORN, THAWED

6 TABLESPOONS BUTTER OR MARGARINE, MELTED

2 JALAPEÑO CHILES, SEEDS AND MEMBRANES DISCARDED, FINELY CHOPPED

1 Preheat oven to 450°F. Grease 13" by 9" metal baking pan.

2 In large bowl, combine flour, cornmeal, sugar, baking powder, baking soda, and salt. In medium bowl, with wire whisk or fork, beat buttermilk and eggs until blended.

3 Add corn, melted butter, and jalapeños to buttermilk mixture; then add to flour mixture. Stir until ingredients are just mixed.

4 Pour batter into prepared pan. Bake 22 to 25 minutes or until golden at edges and toothpick inserted in center comes out clean. Cut lengthwise into 4 strips, then cut each strip crosswise into 6 pieces. Serve warm.

125 CALORIES

PER SERVING. 4G PROTEIN | 19G CARBOHYDRATE | 4G TOTAL FAT (2G SATURATED) 1G FIBER | 36MG CHOLESTEROL | 255MG SODIUM ♥ 🍴

WHOLE-WHEAT SESAME BISCUITS

We blended whole-wheat flour with toasted sesame seeds to make these light golden rounds.

ACTIVE TIME: 15 MINUTES · **TOTAL TIME:** 30 MINUTES
MAKES: 12 BISCUITS

---

2 TABLESPOONS SESAME SEEDS	¾ TEASPOON SALT
1 CUP WHOLE-WHEAT FLOUR	4 TABLESPOONS COLD BUTTER OR MARGARINE
1 CUP ALL-PURPOSE FLOUR	¾ CUP PLUS 3 TABLESPOONS MILK
1 TABLESPOON BAKING POWDER	

1 In small skillet, toast sesame seeds over medium heat until lightly browned, about 5 minutes, stirring occasionally.

2 Preheat oven to 425°F. Lightly grease large cookie sheet.

3 In large bowl, mix whole-wheat and all-purpose flours, baking powder, salt, and 5 teaspoons toasted sesame seeds. With pastry blender or two knives used scissor-fashion, cut in butter until mixture resembles coarse crumbs. Stir in ¾ cup plus 2 tablespoons milk, stirring just until mixture forms a soft dough that leaves sides of bowl.

4 Turn dough onto lightly floured surface; knead 8 to 10 strokes to mix thoroughly. With floured rolling pin, roll dough ½ inch thick

5 With floured 2½-inch round biscuit cutter, cut out biscuits. Place biscuits about 2 inches apart on cookie sheet. Press trimmings together; roll out and cut again.

6 Brush tops of biscuits with remaining 1 tablespoon milk; sprinkle with remaining 1 teaspoon sesame seeds. Bake until golden, 12 to 15 minutes.

---

125 CALORIES

PER BISCUIT. 3G PROTEIN | 17G CARBOHYDRATE | 6G TOTAL FAT (1G SATURATED)
2G FIBER | 3MG CHOLESTEROL | 285MG SODIUM ♥

WHEAT-BERRY SALAD WITH DRIED CHERRIES

This salad is a wonderful mix of textures and flavors: Chewy, nutty wheat berries, tart dried cherries, and crunchy celery are dressed with a sweet and tangy vinaigrette.

ACTIVE TIME: 15 MINUTES · **TOTAL TIME:** 1 HOUR 45 MINUTES
MAKES: 12 SIDE-DISH SERVINGS

---

2 CUPS WHEAT BERRIES (WHOLE-WHEAT KERNELS)

8 CUPS WATER

1 LARGE SHALLOT, MINCED

3 TABLESPOONS FRESH LEMON JUICE

1 TABLESPOON DIJON MUSTARD

1 TABLESPOON OLIVE OIL

2 TEASPOONS HONEY OR AGAVE NECTAR (SEE TIP, PAGE 114)

1½ TEASPOONS SALT

½ TEASPOON COARSELY GROUND BLACK PEPPER

3 STALKS CELERY, CUT INTO ¼-INCH DICE

¾ CUP DRIED TART CHERRIES, CHOPPED

½ CUP CHOPPED FRESH FLAT-LEAF PARSLEY PLUS ADDITIONAL SPRIGS FOR GARNISH

LETTUCE LEAVES

---

1   In 4-quart saucepan, heat wheat berries and water to boiling over high heat. Reduce heat to low; cover and simmer until wheat berries are just tender but still firm to the bite, about 1½ hours.

2   Meanwhile, in large bowl, with wire whisk or fork, mix shallot, lemon juice, mustard, oil, honey, salt, and pepper.

3   When wheat berries are cooked, drain well. Add warm wheat berries to dressing with celery, cherries, and chopped parsley; toss well. Serve salad on lettuce leaves at room temperature, or cover and refrigerate until ready to serve. Garnish with parsley sprigs.

 130 CALORIES

PER SERVING. 4G PROTEIN | 26G CARBOHYDRATE | 2G TOTAL FAT (0G SATURATED) 6G FIBER | 0MG CHOLESTEROL | 310MG SODIUM

BRAN MUFFINS

These healthful fiber-packed muffins are sweetly flavored with a hint of molasses. Try our tasty banana and toasted wheat germ variation.

ACTIVE TIME: 15 MINUTES · TOTAL TIME: 35 MINUTES
MAKES: 12 MUFFINS

1½ CUPS ORIGINAL WHOLE-BRAN
    CEREAL (NOT BRAN FLAKES)

1   CUP LOW-FAT MILK (1%)

¼   CUP VEGETABLE OIL

¼   CUP LIGHT (MILD) MOLASSES

1   LARGE EGG

1   CUP ALL-PURPOSE FLOUR

¼   CUP SUGAR

2   TEASPOONS BAKING POWDER

½   TEASPOON SALT

¼   TEASPOON BAKING SODA

1   Preheat oven to 400°F. Grease twelve 2½-inch muffin-pan cups.

2   In medium bowl, with fork, mix bran cereal with milk, oil, molasses, and egg until blended; let stand 10 minutes.

3   Meanwhile, in large bowl, combine flour, sugar, baking powder, salt, and baking soda.

4   Add liquid mixture to flour mixture; stir just until flour is evenly moistened. Spoon batter into prepared muffin-pan cups.

5   Bake until toothpick inserted in center of muffin comes out clean, 18 to 20 minutes. Immediately remove muffins from pan. Serve warm, or cool on wire rack to serve later.

140 CALORIES — **PER MUFFIN.** 3G PROTEIN | 22G CARBOHYDRATE | 6G TOTAL FAT (1G SATURATED) 3G FIBER | 19MG CHOLESTEROL | 205MG SODIUM ♥ ▭

BANANA–WHEAT GERM BRAN MUFFINS

Prepare Bran Muffins as instructed above but use only **¾ cup milk,** add **¼ teaspoon ground cinnamon** to flour mixture, and fold **1 mashed medium banana (about ½ cup)** and **2 tablespoons honey-toasted wheat germ** into batter before spooning into muffin cups.

150 CALORIES — **PER MUFFIN.** 4G PROTEIN | 25G CARBOHYDRATE | 6G TOTAL FAT (1G SATURATED) 4G FIBER | 18MG CHOLESTEROL | 205MG SODIUM ♥ ▭

PEACH, CUCUMBER, AND BARLEY SALAD

Juicy, just-picked peaches play off the pearl barley, garbanzo beans, and cucumbers in this filling, supper-worthy salad. Double the portion and serve over a bed of Boston lettuce leaves for a colorful and cooling meal. For photo, see page 122.

ACTIVE TIME: 20 MINUTES · TOTAL TIME: 50 MINUTES
MAKES: 10 FIRST-COURSE SERVINGS

---

1   CUP PEARL BARLEY

1   CAN (14½ OUNCES) REDUCED-SODIUM VEGETABLE BROTH OR 1¾ CUPS HOMEMADE BROTH (PAGE 37)

1¼ CUPS WATER

2   TABLESPOONS CIDER VINEGAR

1   TABLESPOON VEGETABLE OIL

¼   TEASPOON SALT

1   ENGLISH (SEEDLESS) CUCUMBER, CHOPPED INTO ¼-INCH PIECES

2   RIPE PEACHES, CHOPPED INTO ¼-INCH PIECES

2   PINTS CHERRY TOMATOES, CUT INTO QUARTERS

½   CUP PACKED FRESH BASIL LEAVES, VERY FINELY CHOPPED

1   CAN (15-OUNCE) CHICKPEAS (GARBANZO BEANS), RINSED AND DRAINED

1   HEAD BOSTON LETTUCE, LEAVES SEPARATED

---

1   Place barley in 4-quart saucepan. Cook over medium heat 5 minutes or until toasted, stirring. Stir in broth and water. Heat to boiling over high heat. Cover, reduce heat to low, and simmer 35 minutes or until tender. Drain if necessary and cool slightly.

2   Meanwhile, in large bowl, whisk vinegar, oil, and salt. Add barley and toss until well coated. Cool until no longer hot, then add cucumber, peaches, tomatoes, basil, and chickpeas, tossing until well combined. Serve over lettuce leaves.

145 CALORIES

PER SERVING. 5G PROTEIN | 28G CARBOHYDRATE | 2G TOTAL FAT (0G SATURATED) 6G FIBER | 0MG CHOLESTEROL | 206MG SODIUM Ⓥ ♥ ⓦ

MILLET WITH CORN AND GREEN CHILES

Millet has a mild flavor that is greatly enhanced by pan-toasting it first. For an extra shot of flavor, serve this topped with a dollop of nonfat Greek yogurt and your favorite salsa.

ACTIVE TIME: 15 MINUTES · TOTAL TIME: 50 MINUTES PLUS STANDING
MAKES: 8 SIDE-DISH SERVINGS

1   CUP MILLET

2   CUPS FRESH CORN KERNELS (CUT FROM 4 EARS) OR FROZEN CORN KERNELS

2   TEASPOONS VEGETABLE OIL

1   MEDIUM ONION, CHOPPED

1   GARLIC CLOVE, CRUSHED WITH GARLIC PRESS

1   TEASPOON GROUND CUMIN

3½ CUPS WATER

1   CAN (4½ OUNCES) DICED GREEN CHILES, DRAINED

½   TEASPOON SALT

¼   CUP LIGHTLY PACKED FRESH CILANTRO LEAVES, CHOPPED (OPTIONAL)

1   In large skillet, toast millet over medium heat, about 5 minutes, stirring frequently. Pour millet into bowl and set aside.

2   Add corn to dry skillet and cook over high heat until corn browns, about 5 minutes, stirring frequently. Transfer corn to plate.

3   In same skillet, heat oil over medium heat. Add onion; cook until softened, about 5 minutes. Stir in garlic and cumin and cook until fragrant, about 1 minute. Add water, green chiles, and salt. Heat to boiling. Stir in millet. Reduce heat; cover and simmer until millet is tender and water is absorbed, 25 to 30 minutes.

4   Remove skillet from heat, stir in corn; cover and let stand 5 minutes to heat through. Stir in cilantro if using.

150 CALORIES

PER SERVING. 4G PROTEIN | 29G CARBOHYDRATE | 3G TOTAL FAT (0G SATURATED) 4G FIBER | 0MG CHOLESTEROL | 200MG SODIUM ♥ ♥ ▦

CHUNKY VEGETABLE BULGUR SALAD

Reminiscent of tabbouleh, this healthy whole-grain salad also contains cherry tomatoes and two kinds of summer squash.

ACTIVE TIME: 20 MINUTES · TOTAL TIME: 20 MINUTES PLUS STANDING
MAKES: 8 SIDE-DISH SERVINGS

2   CUPS BULGUR

2½ CUPS BOILING WATER

2   LEMONS

1   TABLESPOON OLIVE OIL

1   SMALL RED ONION, FINELY CHOPPED

1   CUP CHERRY TOMATOES, EACH CUT IN HALF

1   MEDIUM ZUCCHINI (8 TO 10 OUNCES), CHOPPED

1   MEDIUM YELLOW SUMMER SQUASH (8 TO 10 OUNCES), CHOPPED

½   CUP LOOSELY PACKED FRESH MINT LEAVES, CHOPPED

½   CUP LOOSELY PACKED FRESH PARSLEY LEAVES, CHOPPED

½   TEASPOON SALT

¼   TEASPOON COARSELY GROUND BLACK PEPPER

1   In large bowl, stir together bulgur and boiling water. Cover and let stand until liquid is absorbed, about 30 minutes.

2   Meanwhile, from lemons, grate 1 teaspoon peel and squeeze ¼ cup juice; set aside.

3   In 12-inch skillet, heat oil over medium-high heat until hot. Add onion and cook until it begins to soften, 3 to 4 minutes. Add tomatoes, zucchini, and squash, and cook until vegetables are tender, 6 to 8 minutes, stirring occasionally.

4   Stir vegetables into bulgur with lemon peel and juice, mint, parsley, salt, and pepper. If not serving right away, refrigerate in airtight container up to 1 day.

160 CALORIES

PER SERVING. 6G PROTEIN | 32G CARBOHYDRATE | 2G TOTAL FAT (0G SATURATED) 8G FIBER | 0MG CHOLESTEROL | 160MG SODIUM ♥ ♥ ◉ ☰

POPOVERS

These irresistible rolls are crispy on the outside and hollow on the inside. Serve them fresh from the oven as an accompaniment or fill with one of our grain or green salads. You can make them ahead and reheat in a 400°F oven for 15 minutes.

ACTIVE TIME: 10 MINUTES · TOTAL TIME: 1 HOUR 10 MINUTES
MAKES: 8 POPOVERS

3   LARGE EGGS

1   CUP MILK

3   TABLESPOONS BUTTER OR
    MARGARINE, MELTED

1   CUP ALL-PURPOSE FLOUR

½   TEASPOON SALT

1   Preheat oven to 375°F. Generously grease eight 6-ounce custard cups or twelve 2½" by 1¼" muffin-pan cups with butter or vegetable oil. Place custard cups in jelly-roll pan for easier handling.

2   In blender, combine eggs, milk, butter, flour, and salt; blend until smooth.

3   Pour about ⅓ cup batter into each prepared custard cup, or fill muffin-pan cups half full. Bake 50 minutes, then, with tip of knife, quickly cut small slit in top of each popover to release steam; bake 10 minutes longer. Immediately remove popovers from cups, loosening with spatula if necessary. Serve hot.

160
CALORIES

EACH POPOVER. 5G PROTEIN | 14G CARBOHYDRATE | 9G TOTAL FAT (5G SATURATED) 0G FIBER | 101MG CHOLESTEROL | 247MG SODIUM

COUSCOUS FOUR WAYS

Couscous, or Moroccan pasta, is the perfect side for a busy weekday meal, taking all of ten minutes to put together from start to finish. It's satisfying as is, but it only takes another couple of minutes to put your own personal spin on it. Try one of our three flavor variations, then let your own imagination guide you. Start with 1 cup of whole-wheat couscous and prepare it according to package instructions, but omit any added butter. Makes 4 side-dish servings.

170
CALORIES

PER SERVING. 7G PROTEIN | 37G CARBOHYDRATE | 0G TOTAL FAT | 6G FIBER 0MG CHOLESTEROL | 290MG SODIUM ✓ Ⓥ ♥ 🌱

LIME COUSCOUS

Add **1 tablespoon fresh lime juice** and **1 teaspoon freshly grated lime peel** to water when preparing couscous.

170
CALORIES

PER SERVING. 7G PROTEIN | 37G CARBOHYDRATE | 0G TOTAL FAT | 6G FIBER 0MG CHOLESTEROL | 290MG SODIUM ✓ Ⓥ ♥ 🌱

SUN-DRIED TOMATO AND GREEN ONION COUSCOUS

Add **1 sliced medium green onion** and **5 chopped sun-dried tomato halves** to water when preparing couscous.

180
CALORIES

PER SERVING. 7G PROTEIN | 38G CARBOHYDRATE | 1G TOTAL FAT (0G SATU-RATED) | 6G FIBER | 0MG CHOLESTEROL | 300MG SODIUM ✓ Ⓥ ♥ 🌱

MOROCCAN COUSCOUS

Add ¼ cup golden raisins, ¼ teaspoon ground cinnamon, ¼ teaspoon ground turmeric, and ¼ teaspoon ground cumin to water when preparing couscous.

205
CALORIES

PER SERVING. 7G PROTEIN | 45G CARBOHYDRATE | 1G TOTAL FAT (0G SATU-RATED) | 7G FIBER | 0MG CHOLESTEROL | 290MG SODIUM ✓ Ⓥ ♥ 🌱

WHOLE-GRAIN BLUEBERRY MUFFINS

Deliciously dense, these muffins are made with a combination of regular all-purpose flour, whole-wheat flour, and old-fashioned oats for the optimum blend of flavor and healthful benefits.

ACTIVE TIME: 20 MINUTES · TOTAL TIME: 40 MINUTES

MAKES: 12 MUFFINS

---

1 CUP OLD-FASHIONED OATS, UNCOOKED	1 CUP LOW-FAT BUTTERMILK
1 CUP WHOLE-WHEAT FLOUR	¼ CUP FRESH ORANGE JUICE
½ CUP ALL-PURPOSE FLOUR	2 TABLESPOONS CANOLA OIL
2 TEASPOONS BAKING POWDER	1 LARGE EGG
½ TEASPOON BAKING SODA	1 TEASPOON VANILLA EXTRACT
½ TEASPOON SALT	2 CUPS BLUEBERRIES
5 TABLESPOONS PACKED BROWN SUGAR	¼ CUP NATURAL ALMONDS, CHOPPED

1 Preheat oven to 400°F. Line 12-cup muffin pan with paper liners.

2 Grind oats in blender. In bowl, whisk oats, flours, baking powder and soda, salt, and ¼ cup sugar. In small bowl, whisk buttermilk, juice, oil, egg, and vanilla. Stir into flour mixture; fold in blueberries.

3 Combine nuts and remaining 1 tablespoon sugar. Spoon batter into pan; sprinkle with almond sugar. Bake 22 minutes or until toothpick inserted in center of muffin comes out clean. Cool in pan on wire rack 5 minutes. Remove from pan; cool completely.

170 CALORIES

PER MUFFIN. 5G PROTEIN | 28G CARBOHYDRATE | 5G TOTAL FAT (1G SATURATED) 3G FIBER | 16MG CHOLESTEROL | 270MG SODIUM ♥ 🛒

130
CALORIES
Peachy Frozen Yogurt
(page 141)

SWEET & FRUITY TREATS

We've decided to put the spotlight on fruit because, in general, fruit is high in vitamin C and a good source of dietary fiber. And, if you eat fruits in season throughout the year, you'll get a rotating roster of nutritional highs—including a range of vitamins and antioxidants—and satisfy your sweet tooth, too. For your dessert add-ons, enjoy fresh fruit sliced in a parfait or fruit salad, dried fruit mixed into cookies, or apples and bananas broiled or baked. Or for something new, sample our pretty-in-pink Watermelon Slushie or our delectable Stuffed Fresh Figs.

KEY TO ICONS

🕐 30 minutes or less   Ⓥ Vegan   ♥ Heart healthy   🌾 High fiber   🍴 Make ahead

CHOCOLATE-ALMOND MERINGUES

These dainty meringues are dipped first in bittersweet chocolate, then in roasted salted almonds. The results? Heavenly.

ACTIVE TIME: 40 MINUTES · TOTAL TIME: 2 HOURS 10 MINUTES PLUS STANDING
MAKES: ABOUT 54 COOKIES

---

3 LARGE EGG WHITES

¼ TEASPOON ALMOND EXTRACT

⅛ TEASPOON CREAM OF TARTAR

PINCH SALT

½ CUP SUGAR

¾ CUP ROASTED SALTED ALMONDS

5 SQUARES (5 OUNCES) BITTERSWEET CHOCOLATE, CHOPPED

1 Preheat oven to 200°F. Line two cookie sheets with parchment paper.

2 In medium bowl, with mixer on high speed, beat egg whites, almond extract, cream of tartar, and salt until soft peaks form. With mixer running, sprinkle in sugar, 2 tablespoons at a time, beating until sugar dissolves and meringue stands in stiff, glossy peaks when beaters are lifted.

3 Spoon meringue into large decorating bag fitted with ¾-inch round tip, or into large zip-tight plastic bag with small hole cut in one corner. Pipe meringue into 1-inch rounds, about 1 inch apart, on prepared cookie sheets.

4 Bake until crisp but not brown, 1 hour 30 minutes to 1 hour 40 minutes, rotating cookie sheets between upper and lower oven racks halfway through.

5 Cool meringues completely on cookie sheets on wire racks.

6 Meanwhile, in food processor, pulse almonds until chopped; place on plate. In small microwave-safe bowl, microwave chocolate on Medium for 1 minute 30 seconds or until melted, stirring every 30 seconds.

7 Line large jelly-roll pan with parchment paper. Dip bottom third of each meringue in chocolate, then almonds. Place meringues on prepared pan; let stand until set, about 1 hour.

8 Store cookies, with waxed paper between layers, in airtight container at room temperature up to 3 days or in freezer up to 1 month.

---

35 CALORIES

PER COOKIE. 1G PROTEIN | 4G CARBOHYDRATE | 2G TOTAL FAT (1G SATURATED) 0G FIBER | 0MG CHOLESTEROL | 10MG SODIUM ♥ 🍽

HEALTHY MAKEOVER OATMEAL-RAISIN COOKIES

If you thought the words "delicious" and "low-fat" could never be used to describe the same cookie, think again. This one's chewy and sweet, yet it has only 2 grams of fat per cookie.

ACTIVE TIME: 15 MINUTES · TOTAL TIME: 10 MINUTES PER BATCH
MAKES: ABOUT 48 COOKIES

2 CUPS ALL-PURPOSE FLOUR	2 LARGE EGG WHITES
1 TEASPOON BAKING SODA	1 LARGE EGG
½ TEASPOON SALT	2 TEASPOONS VANILLA EXTRACT
½ CUP (1 STICK) LIGHT CORN-OIL SPREAD (56 TO 60% FAT)	1 CUP QUICK-COOKING OATS, UNCOOKED
¾ CUP PACKED DARK BROWN SUGAR	½ CUP DARK SEEDLESS RAISINS
½ CUP GRANULATED SUGAR	

1   Preheat oven to 375°F. Grease two large cookie sheets. In medium bowl, combine flour, baking soda, and salt.

2   In large bowl, with mixer at low speed, beat corn-oil spread and both sugars until well combined. Increase speed to high; beat until mixture is light and fluffy. Add egg whites, whole egg, and vanilla; beat until blended. With wooden spoon, stir in flour mixture, oats, and raisins until combined.

3   Drop dough by level tablespoons, 2 inches apart, on prepared cookie sheets. Bake until golden, 10 to 12 minutes, rotating cookie sheets between upper and lower oven racks halfway through. With wide spatula, transfer cookies to wire racks to cool completely.

4   Repeat with remaining dough.

PER COOKIE. 1G PROTEIN | 12G CARBOHYDRATE | 2G TOTAL FAT (0G SATURATED) 0G FIBER | 4MG CHOLESTEROL | 72MG SODIUM ♥ ▭

65 CALORIES

SLICED CITRUS WITH LIME SYRUP

Served on top of plain or vanilla yogurt, this versatile fruit dish is fabulous for breakfast or dessert. It's also a fun addition to a brunch buffet.

ACTIVE TIME: 20 MINUTES · TOTAL TIME: 25 MINUTES PLUS CHILLING

MAKES: 6 SERVINGS

From **1 or 2 lemons,** grate 1 teaspoon peel and squeeze 3 tablespoons juice. From **1 lime,** grate ½ teaspoon peel and squeeze 1 tablespoon juice. In 1-quart saucepan, combine juices and ½ **cup sugar**; heat to boiling over medium-high heat. Reduce heat to low; simmer 1 minute. Stir in lemon and lime peels, cover, and refrigerate until cold. Meanwhile, cut peel and white pith from **2 navel oranges, 2 clementines,** and **2 red or white grapefruit.** Slice all fruit crosswise into ¼-inch-thick rounds. Arrange slices on deep large platter. Spoon syrup over fruit. If not serving right away, cover and refrigerate up to 2 days.

95 CALORIES

PER SERVING. 1G PROTEIN | 24G CARBOHYDRATE | 0G TOTAL FAT | 3G FIBER | 0MG CHOLESTEROL | 1MG SODIUM ♥ Ⓥ 🍱

BERRIES IN RED WINE

A delectable summer dessert—mixed berries steeped in a sweet, cinnamon-scented red-wine syrup.

TOTAL TIME: 15 MINUTES PLUS CHILLING

MAKES: 5 CUPS OR 6 SERVINGS

In 1-quart saucepan, heat **⅓ cup sugar, 1 (3-inch-long) stick cinnamon,** and **½ cup red wine** such as Shiraz or Zinfandel to boiling over medium-high heat. Boil 2 minutes. Place **1 pound hulled strawberries** and **1 pint raspberries** in medium bowl. Pour **1½ cups wine** and wine mixture over berries. Cover mixture and refrigerate 1 to 3 hours to blend flavors. To serve, ladle berries with syrup into wine goblets or dessert bowls.

125 CALORIES **PER SERVING.** 1G PROTEIN | 22G CARBOHYDRATE | 1G TOTAL FAT (0G SATURATED) 4G FIBER | 0MG CHOLESTEROL | 5MG SODIUM

PEACHY FROZEN YOGURT

Served as a fruity dessert or snack, our creamy Peachy Frozen Yogurt delivers a double dose of peach flavor and only 1 gram of fat per serving. For photo, see page 136. This formula works with other frozen fruit and fruit yogurt combos too—try cherry, raspberry, or strawberry.

TOTAL TIME: 5 MINUTES

MAKES: 2½ CUPS OR 4 SERVINGS

In food processor with knife blade attached, process **1 bag frozen sliced peaches (10 to 12 ounces)** until finely shaved. Add **2 containers (6 ounces each) low-fat peach yogurt** and **1 tablespoon sugar.** Process just until smooth. Serve immediately or, if not serving right away, pour into 9-inch square baking pan; cover and freeze no longer than 1 hour for best texture.

130 CALORIES **PER SERVING.** 4G PROTEIN | 28G CARBOHYDRATE | 1G TOTAL FAT (1G SATURATED) 2G FIBER | 6MG CHOLESTEROL | 50MG SODIUM

BANANA BERRY PARFAITS

This quick dessert looks sensational in an old-fashioned sundae glass.

TOTAL TIME: 10 MINUTES

MAKES: 4 SERVINGS

1¼ CUPS UNSWEETENED FROZEN RASPBERRIES, PARTIALLY THAWED

1   TABLESPOON SUGAR

2⅔ CUPS FAT-FREE VANILLA YOGURT

2   RIPE BANANAS, PEELED AND THINLY SLICED

FRESH RASPBERRIES FOR GARNISH (OPTIONAL)

1   In food processor with knife blade attached, pulse thawed raspberries and sugar until almost smooth.

2   Into four 10-ounce glasses or goblets, layer about half of berry puree, half of yogurt, and half of banana slices; repeat layering. Top with fresh raspberries, if you like.

140 CALORIES

PER SERVING. 6G PROTEIN | 30G CARBOHYDRATE | 0G TOTAL FAT (0G SATURATED) 2G FIBER | 3MG CHOLESTEROL | 95MG SODIUM 🖤

THREE-FRUIT SALAD WITH VANILLA SYRUP

Perfect alone or alongside pound cake. If you don't have a vanilla bean, stir ½ teaspoon vanilla extract into the chilled syrup.

ACTIVE TIME: 30 MINUTES · TOTAL TIME: 40 MINUTES PLUS CHILLING

MAKES: 12 SERVINGS

Use vegetable peeler to remove 1-inch-wide continuous strip of peel from **1 lemon,** then squeeze ¼ cup juice (**another lemon** may be needed). Cut **1 vanilla bean** lengthwise in half. With small knife, scrape seeds into 1-quart saucepan; drop pod into pan. Add lemon peel and ¾ **cup each water and sugar**; heat to boiling over high heat. Reduce heat to medium and cook until syrup thickens slightly, about 5 minutes. Pour mixture through sieve into small bowl; stir in lemon juice. Cover and refrigerate until chilled, about 2 hours. Peel and seed **3 ripe mangoes** and **1 medium honeydew** and cut into 1-inch pieces; hull **2 pints strawberries** and cut each in half or into quarters if large. Place fruit in large bowl, add syrup, and toss.

140 CALORIES

PER SERVING. 1G PROTEIN | 35G CARBOHYDRATE | 0G TOTAL FAT | 3G FIBER 0MG CHOLESTEROL | 13MG SODIUM 🖤 Ⓥ

BROILED BROWN-SUGAR BANANAS

A sweet, satisfying dessert with just four basic ingredients.

ACTIVE TIME: 5 MINUTES · TOTAL TIME: 10 MINUTES
MAKES: 4 SERVINGS

Preheat broiler and place rack close to heat source. Cut **4 bananas,** with peels still on, almost in half lengthwise, taking care not to cut all the way through and leaving 1 inch uncut at ends. In cup, with fork, blend **2 tablespoons packed brown sugar, 1 tablespoon reduced-fat margarine,** and **⅛ teaspoon ground cinnamon.** Place bananas, cut side up, on rack in broiling pan. Spoon sugar mixture over split bananas. Broil until browned, about 5 minutes. Serve in skins and use spoon to scoop out fruit.

150 CALORIES **PER SERVING.** 1G PROTEIN | 34G CARBOHYDRATE | 2G TOTAL FAT (1G SATURATED) 3G FIBER | 0MG CHOLESTEROL | 20MG SODIUM ♥ ♥ ♥

STUFFED FRESH FIGS

Figs are a good source of dietary fiber and potassium, as well as being one of the best sources of phytosterols, plant nutrients that have been shown to help reduce cholesterol levels. And did we mention that they're delicious? When you're lucky enough to find ripe figs in your market, be sure to try this recipe.

TOTAL TIME: 25 MINUTES
MAKES: 6 SERVINGS

19 SMALL FRESH RIPE FIGS
    (1¼ POUNDS; SEE TIP)

¼ CUP HONEY

½ CUP PART-SKIM RICOTTA CHEESE

¼ CUP NATURAL ALMONDS,
    TOASTED AND CHOPPED

1   On plate, with fork, mash ripest fig with honey; set aside.

2   With sharp knife, trim stems from remaining figs, then cut a deep X in top of each, making sure not to cut through to bottom. With fingertips, gently spread each fig apart to make "petals."

3   In small bowl, combine ricotta and almonds. With back of spoon, press mashed fig-and-honey mixture through sieve into 1-cup measure.

4   To serve, spoon ricotta mixture into figs. Arrange figs on platter. Drizzle with fig honey.

TIP The season for fresh figs is short, and they're expensive, so if you indulge in them, be sure to get your money's worth. Buy fruit that is heavy, smells fresh (not musty), and is soft to the touch. Use promptly; figs will keep, refrigerated, for only a day or two. Rinse figs gently before using them. The entire fruit is edible, skin and all—just discard the stem.

170 CALORIES

PER SERVING. 4G PROTEIN | 32G CARBOHYDRATE | 4G TOTAL FAT (1G SATURATED) 4G FIBER | 6MG CHOLESTEROL | 25MG SODIUM 💚 🖤

MEYER LEMON PUDDING CAKES

Meyer lemons, now available in most supermarkets, give this dessert its sweet-tart taste. The lemons also help create the light layers—since the acid in the juice can't bind with the egg whites, the dish divides into a citrusy cake and a creamy custard.

ACTIVE TIME: 25 MINUTES · TOTAL TIME: 1 HOUR PLUS COOLING
MAKES: 8 CAKES

¾ CUP SUGAR

¼ CUP ALL-PURPOSE FLOUR

¼ TEASPOON SALT

2 MEYER LEMONS OR 3 REGULAR LEMONS

3 LARGE EGGS, SEPARATED

2 TABLESPOONS BUTTER OR MARGARINE, MELTED AND COOLED

1 CUP WHOLE MILK

1 PINT RASPBERRIES FOR GARNISH

8 FRESH MINT SPRIGS FOR GARNISH

1   Preheat oven to 350°F. Grease eight 4- to 5-ounce ramekins; using 1 teaspoon sugar per ramekin, coat bottom and sides; shake out excess.

2   On sheet of waxed paper, with fork, combine flour, ⅓ cup sugar, and salt. From lemons, grate 1½ tablespoons peel and squeeze ½ cup juice. In large bowl, with wire whisk, beat egg yolks and lemon peel and juice. Whisk in butter and milk. Gradually whisk in flour mixture.

3   In another large bowl, with mixer on medium speed, beat egg whites until foamy. Gradually beat in remaining ¼ cup sugar until soft peaks form when beaters are lifted, 2 to 3 minutes.

4   Add one-third beaten whites to yolk mixture and, with rubber spatula, stir gently until incorporated. Gently fold in remaining whites until just incorporated. With ladle, divide batter evenly among prepared ramekins.

5   Arrange ramekins 1 inch apart in large (17" by 13") roasting pan. Fill pan with enough *hot water* to come halfway up sides of ramekins. Carefully transfer pan to oven and bake 30 to 35 minutes or until cakes are golden brown and tops rise ½ inch above rims.

6   Cool cakes in pan on wire rack 5 minutes. With sturdy metal spatula, carefully remove ramekins from pan with water and transfer to wire rack to cool 15 minutes longer.

7   Run thin knife around edge of 1 ramekin. Place small serving plate on top of ramekin and invert plate and ramekin together; remove ramekin. Repeat with remaining ramekins. Garnish each cake with a few raspberries and a mint sprig; serve warm.

170
CALORIES

PER SERVING. 4G PROTEIN | 25G CARBOHYDRATE | 6G TOTAL FAT (3G SATURATED)
3G FIBER | 92MG CHOLESTEROL | 145MG SODIUM ♥ ▭

WATERMELON SLUSHIE

We combined antioxidant-rich pomegranate juice with fresh watermelon and ice to create this ruby-red summer cooler.

TOTAL TIME: 5 MINUTES

MAKES: 1 SERVING

In blender, combine **2 cups 1-inch pieces seedless watermelon, ½ cup pomegranate juice,** and **½ cup ice cubes**. Blend until smooth. Pour into tall glass.

PER 2-CUP SERVING. 2G PROTEIN | 40G CARBOHYDRATE | 1G TOTAL FAT | 2G FIBER 0MG CHOLESTEROL | 10MG SODIUM ❤ ⓥ ♥

APPLE-OAT CRISP

This crisp works beautifully with either tart Granny Smith apples or the sweeter Golden Delicious variety; both hold their shape nicely when baked. Our test kitchen staff prefers a combination of the two.

ACTIVE TIME: 15 MINUTES · TOTAL TIME: 45 MINUTES
MAKES: 12 SERVINGS

1 LEMON

3 POUNDS GRANNY SMITH AND/OR GOLDEN DELICIOUS APPLES, PEELED, CORED, AND CUT INTO 1-INCH WEDGES

⅓ CUP PLUS ¼ CUP PACKED LIGHT BROWN SUGAR

2 TABLESPOONS PLUS ⅓ CUP ALL-PURPOSE FLOUR

1 TEASPOON GROUND CINNAMON

½ TEASPOON SALT

1 CUP OLD-FASHIONED OATS, UNCOOKED

4 TABLESPOONS BUTTER OR MARGARINE, SOFTENED

1 Preheat oven to 425°F. From lemon, grate ½ teaspoon peel and squeeze 2 tablespoons juice. In 13" by 9" glass or ceramic baking dish, toss lemon peel and juice with apple wedges, ⅓ cup brown sugar, 2 tablespoons flour, cinnamon, and salt until apples are evenly coated.

2 In medium bowl, mix oats with remaining ¼ cup sugar and ⅓ cup flour. With fingertips, blend in butter until mixture resembles coarse crumbs. Press crumb mixture into clumps and sprinkle over apple mixture.

3 Bake apple crisp 30 to 35 minutes or until apples are tender and topping is lightly browned. Cool crisp on wire rack for 10 minutes to serve warm, or cool completely (1 hour) on rack to serve later. Reheat if desired.

175
CALORIES

PER ½-CUP SERVING. 2G PROTEIN | 33G CARBOHYDRATE | 5G TOTAL FAT (3G SATURATED) | 3G FIBER | 11MG CHOLESTEROL | 145MG SODIUM ✓ 🍴

GENERAL INDEX

Note: Page numbers in **bold** indicate recipe category summaries/overviews.

Carrots
    Carrot-Fennel Slaw, 32
    Ginger Carrot Soup, 34, 41
    Not Your Grandma's
        Vegetable Soup, 43
Casseroles. See Pasta and
    casseroles
Cauliflower
    Cauliflower-Curry
        Stew, 48
    Roasted Cauliflower, 110
Celery root, in Root
    Vegetable Gratin, 116–117
Cereal, five-minute
    multigrain, 88–89
Cheese
    Crustless Tomato-Ricotta
        Pie, 94
    Greens with Goat
        Cheese and Tangerine
        Vinaigrette, 121
    Lasagna Toasts, 22–23
    pizza with. See Pizzas
    Ricotta-Stuffed Peppers,
        58–59
Cherries (dried), wheat-
    berry salad with, 126
Chickpeas. See Beans and
    legumes
Chiles Relleños
    Casserole, 99
Chili, 46–47
Chips, kale, 108
Chocolate-Almond
    Meringues, 138
Chunky Vegetable Bulgur
    Salad, 130–131
Cilantro Cream, 38
Citrus
    Creamy Lemon
        Sauce, 118
    Lime Couscous, 133
    Meyer Lemon Pudding
        Cakes, 146–147
    Sliced Citrus with Lime
        Syrup, 140
    Tangerine Vinaigrette, 121
Corn
    about: cornmeal, 12
    Double Cornbread, 124
    Mexican Veggie Stacks,
        56–57

Polenta Lasagna, 77
Southwestern Frittata, 98
Tostada Stacks, 92–93
Couscous
    about, 12
    Couscous Four Ways, 133
    Couscous-Stuffed
        Artichokes, 60–61
    Lime Couscous, 133
    Moroccan Couscous, 133
    Sun-Dried Tomato
        and Green Onion
        Couscous, 133
Crunchy Peanut
    Broccoli, 119
Crustless Tomato-Ricotta
    Pie, 94
Cucumbers
    Gazpacho with Cilantro
        Cream, 38–39
    Peach, Cucumber, and
        Barley Salad, 122, 128

Dairy substitutes, 14
Desserts. See Sweet, fruity
    treats
Double Cornbread, 124

Eggs
    about: nutritional
        benefits, 96;
        substitutes, 14
    California Breakfast
        Wrap, 86, 91
    Crustless Tomato-Ricotta
        Pie, 94
    Popovers, 132
    Scrambled Eggs with
        Fresh Herbs, 90
    Southwestern Frittata, 98
    Tostada Stacks, 92–93

Farfalle with Baby
    Artichokes and
    Mushrooms, 70–71
Fast Fried Rice, 64
Fennel, in Carrot-Fennel
    Slaw, 32
Fiber, 10
Figs, stuffed fresh, 145
Five-Minute Multigrain
    Cereal, 88–89

Fried dishes. See Stuffed,
    stacked, stir-fried dishes
Fruits. See also specific fruits;
    Sweet, fruity treats
    about: nutritional
        benefits, 15;
        seasonal, 10
    Whole-Grain Pancakes,
        102–103

Garbanzo beans. See Beans
    and legumes
Gazpacho with Cilantro
    Cream, 38–39
Ginger Carrot Soup, 34, 41
Grains, **123–135**. See also
    Breads; Corn; Couscous;
    Oats; Pasta and
    casseroles; Rice
    about: barley, 12; fiber
        and, 10; millet, 12–13;
        nutritional benefits,
        12–13; quinoa, 13;
        wheat, 13
    Bulgur Pilaf with
        Apricots, 80–81
    Chunky Vegetable Bulgur
        Salad, 130–131
    Five-Minute Multigrain
        Cereal, 88–89
    Millet with Corn and
        Green Chiles, 129
    Peach, Cucumber, and
        Barley Salad, 122, 128
    Stuffed Portobellos, 62–63
    Wheat-Berry Salad with
        Dried Cherries, 126
Greek Salad Pitas, 20
Green beans
    Green Beans with Mixed
        Mushrooms, 112–113
    Summer Tomato Risotto,
        84–85
Greens. See also Salads
    Spaghetti with Beets and
        Greens, 74–75
    Vegetable Lasagna, 68, 76
Green Tomato Stacks, 52, 54
Grilled Mexican Pizza,
    26–27
Grilled Vegetable
    Burritos, 25

INDEX OF RECIPES BY ICON

This index makes it easy to search recipes by category, including 30 minutes or less, heart-healthy, high-fiber, make-ahead, and vegan dishes.

❤ HEART HEALTHY

If you're looking for heart-healthy options, look no further. Each main dish contains 5 grams or less saturated fat, 150 milligrams or less cholesterol, and 480 milligrams or less sodium. Each appetizer or side dish contains 2 grams or less saturated fat, 50 milligrams or less cholesterol, and 360 milligrams or less sodium.

🌱 HIGH FIBER

Want to get more fill-you-up fiber into your diet? Incorporate the following high fiber dishes into your regular repertoire. Each of these recipes contains 5 grams or more fiber per serving.

🍲 MAKE AHEAD

For convenience, you can make all (or a portion) of these recipes ahead of time. The individual recipes indicate which steps you can do-ahead or how long you can refrigerate or freeze the completed dish.

Ⓥ VEGAN

Following a diet that's
free of animal products
like dairy and eggs? These
recipes are 100-percent
vegan—and sure to satisfy.

PHOTOGRAPHY CREDITS

Antonis Achilleos: 71, 97, 106
James Baigrie: 42, 52, 57, 80, 89, 101, 108, 130
Monica Buck: 45, 79
Tara Donne: 142
Getty Images: Michael Rosenfeld, 11
Brian Hagiwara: 144
iStockphoto: Alea Image, 12; Andyd, 83; James McQuillan, 139
John Kernick: 116
Yunhee Kim: 102
Rita Maas: 66
Kate Mathis: 31, 34, 47, 58, 68, 86, 118, 124, 136, 148
Ellie Miller: 50
Ted Morrison: 119
Con Poulos: 9, 63, 147
David Prince: 140
Alan Richardson: 74
Kate Sears: 18, 23, 26, 112, 115
Shutterstock: 15
Ann Stratton: 39
Studio D: Philip Friedman, 7, 61
Anna Williams: 6, 85, 92, 122

Front Cover and Spine: Kate Mathis
Back Cover: Kate Mathis (left), Anna Williams (right)

METRIC EQUIVALENTS

The recipes that appear in this cookbook use the standard United States method for measuring liquid and dry or solid ingredients (teaspoons, tablespoons, and cups). The information on this chart is provided to help cooks outside the U.S. successfully use these recipes. All equivalents are approximate.

METRIC EQUIVALENTS FOR DIFFERENT TYPES OF INGREDIENTS

A standard cup measure of a dry or solid ingredient will vary in weight depending on the type of ingredient. A standard cup of liquid is the same volume for any type of liquid. Use the following chart when converting standard cup measures to grams (weight) or milliliters (volume).

Standard Cup	Fine Powder (e.g. flour)	Grain (e.g. rice)	Granular (e.g. sugar)	Liquid Solids (e.g. butter)	Liquid (e.g. milk)
1	140 g	150 g	190 g	200 g	240 ml
¾	105 g	113 g	143 g	150 g	180 ml
⅔	93 g	100 g	125 g	133 g	160 ml
½	70 g	75 g	95 g	100 g	120 ml
⅓	47 g	50 g	63 g	67 g	80 ml
¼	35 g	38 g	48 g	50 g	60 ml
⅛	18 g	19 g	24 g	25 g	30 ml

USEFUL EQUIVALENTS FOR LIQUID INGREDIENTS BY VOLUME

¼ tsp	=					1 ml	
½ tsp	=					2 ml	
1 tsp	=					5 ml	
3 tsp	=	1 tbls	=		½ fl oz	=	15 ml
		2 tbls	=	⅛ cup	=	1 fl oz	=	30 ml
		4 tbls	=	¼ cup	=	2 fl oz	=	60 ml
		5⅓ tbls	=	⅓ cup	=	3 fl oz	=	80 ml
		8 tbls	=	½ cup	=	4 fl oz	=	120 ml
		10⅔ tbls	=	⅔ cup	=	5 fl oz	=	160 ml
		12 tbls	=	¾ cup	=	6 fl oz	=	180 ml
		16 tbls	=	1 cup	=	8 fl oz	=	240 ml
		1 pt	=	2 cups	=	16 fl oz	=	480 ml
		1 qt	=	4 cups	=	32 fl oz	=	960 ml
						33 fl oz	=	1000 ml	= 1 L

USEFUL EQUIVALENTS FOR COOKING/OVEN TEMPERATURES

	Fahrenheit	Celsius	Gas Mark
Freeze Water	32° F	0° C	
Room Temperature	68° F	20° C	
Boil Water	212° F	100° C	
Bake	325° F	160° C	3
	350° F	180° C	4
	375° F	190° C	5
	400° F	200° C	6
	425° F	220° C	7
	450° F	230° C	8
Broil			Grill

USEFUL EQUIVALENTS FOR DRY INGREDIENTS BY WEIGHT

(To convert ounces to grams, multiply the number of ounces by 30.)

1 oz	=	¹⁄₁₆ lb	=	30 g
2 oz	=	¼ lb	=	120 g
4 oz	=	½ lb	=	240 g
8 oz	=	¾ lb	=	360 g
16 oz	=	1 lb	=	480 g

USEFUL EQUIVALENTS LENGTH

(To convert inches to centimeters, multiply the number of inches by 2.5.)

1 in =	2.5 cm	
6 in = ½ ft =	15 cm	
12 in = 1 ft =	30 cm	
36 in = 3 ft = 1 yd	= 90 cm	
40 in =	100 cm	= 1 m

THE GOOD HOUSEKEEPING TRIPLE-TEST PROMISE

At *Good Housekeeping*, we want to make sure that every recipe we print works in any oven, with any brand of ingredient, no matter what. That's why, in our test kitchens at the **Good Housekeeping Research Institute,** we go all out: We test each recipe at least three times—and, often, several more times after that.

When a recipe is first developed, one member of our team prepares the dish and we judge it on these criteria: It must be **delicious, family-friendly, healthy,** and **easy to make.**

1 The recipe is then tested several more times to fine-tune the flavor and ease of preparation, always by the same team member, using the same equipment.

2 Next, another team member follows the recipe as written, **varying the brands of ingredients** and **kinds of equipment.** Even the types of stoves we use are changed.

3 A third team member repeats the whole process **using yet another set of equipment** and **alternative ingredients.** By the time the recipes appear in our books, they are guaranteed to work in any kitchen, including yours. **We promise.**